A Level Psychology

Skills Builder

Author: Louise Steans

Acknowledgements

WJEC & Eduqas A Level Psychology – Skills Builder

Published with support from WJEC's Teaching and Learning Resources Scheme

Published in 2019 by WJEC, 245 Western Avenue, Cardiff CF5 2YX

© WJEC 2019

Author: Louise Steans

ISBN: 978-1-86085-707-2

Printed by: KK SOLUTIONS LIMITED

Every effort has been made to contact copyright holders of material reproduced in this book. If notified, the publishers will be pleased to rectify any errors or omissions at the earliest opportunity.

This material has been endorsed by WJEC and offers high quality support for the delivery of WJEC qualifications.

This resource supports the teaching and learning of A Level Psychology. The book addresses psychological exam skills rather than content, and should be used in conjunction with other resources and sound classroom teaching.

To order further copies, please contact: resources@wjec.co.uk

Cover Siphotography / iStock / Getty Images; p.1 onurdongel / iStock / Getty Images; p.23 iMrSquid / DigitalVision / Getty Images; p.31 ANDRZEJ WOJCICKI / Science Photo Library / Getty Images; p.33 SolStock / E+ / Getty Images; p.38 Morsa Images / DigitalVision / Getty Images; p.53 jayk7 / Moment / Getty Images; p.56 Image Source / DigitalVision / Getty Images; p.59 triloks / iStock / Getty Images; p.70 Designed by Freepik; p.83 MARHARYTA MARKO / iStock / Getty Images; p.85 RichVintage / E+ / Getty Images; p.97 PM Images / DigitalVision / Getty Images; p.98 SEAN GLADWELL / Moment / Getty Images; p.101 Dougal Waters / DigitialVision / Getty Images; p.103 baramee2554 / iStock / Getty Images; p.106 Westend61 / Getty Images; p.110 SolStock / iStock / Getty Images; p.122 SIphotography / iStock / Getty Images; p.137 Caiaimage / Tom Merton / Caiaimage / Getty Images; p.145 SolStock / E+ / Getty Images;

Photo acknowledgements

Chapter 1

AO1 Skills: Knowledge and Understanding   1

What is AO1?   2

What should I include in an AO1 answer?   2

Do I need a conclusion in an AO1 question?   28

Taking your knowledge (AO1) beyond the textbook   28

Chapter 2

AO2 Skills: Application of knowledge   33

What is AO2?   34

What should I include in an AO2 answer?   34

Do I need a conclusion in an AO2 question?   35

How does this information fit in with the different exam Units/Components?   36

Chapter 3

AO3 Skills: Evaluation   59

What is AO3?   60

What structure should I use in an AO3 answer?   60

What makes a good evaluation paragraph?   61

How much should I write?   62

What should I write in my conclusion?   62

Chapter 4

Combined AO Questions   85

What is a combined AO question?   86

AO1 and AO3: Contemporary Debates   86

AO1 and AO3: Unit/Component 3 – Section A: Applications   90

AO1/3 and AO2: Unit/Component 3 – Section A: Applications   91

AO2 and AO3: Unit/Component 3 – Section B: Controversies   97

Index

Chapter 5

Questions and Answers   103

Unit/Component 1 – AO1: Classic Research   104

Unit/Component 3 – AO1: Explanations of behaviour   107

Unit/Component 1 – AO2: Applying the assumptions to relationship formation (AS)   111

Component 1 – AO2: Applying the assumptions to behaviour (England Eduqas ONLY)   113

Unit/Component 1 – AO2: Applying the approach to a therapy   116

Unit 2 & 4/Component 2 – AO2: Scenario questions   118

Unit 4 & Component 2 – Applied AO3: Refining your Personal Investigation   124

Unit 4 & Component 2 – AO2: Inferential Statistics   127

Unit/Component 1 – AO3: Evaluate the Classic Research   133

Unit/Component 1 – AO3: Evaluate the Approach   136

Unit/Component 2 – AO3: Social and Developmental Psychology   140

Unit 2/Component 1 – AO1/3: Contemporary Debates   143

Unit/Component 3 – AO2/3: Controversies   148

This book is designed to meet the requirements of the WJEC and Eduqas AS and A level Psychology specifications. The content applies to all units – Psychology: Past to Present (Unit/Component 1), research methods and personal investigations (Unit/Component 2 and Unit 4 in Wales), and implications of psychology in the real world (Unit/Component 3).

The book is thematic, where it addresses psychological exam skills rather than content. Therefore, it is assumed that some basic knowledge of content has already been gained, through lessons or from other more 'traditional' text books. This style has been chosen as the key to success in the 'new specification' for A level Psychology (from 2015) and focusses on HOW you use the information. Rote learning styles (memorisation of information based on repetition) which may have been used successfully in the past, will no longer be sufficient. These skills can be applied in any exam paper, but there are specific examples of question styles and techniques within the main body of the book, and in the questions and answers section at the end. There is also a student workbook that you can use alongside this book to practice the skills you have learned.

Introduction

There are three different ways that you can be assessed in an AS or A level Psychology exam paper. These different skills are referred to as assessment objectives or AOs. The WJEC/Eduqas specifications state the following about the three assessment objectives:

AO1

Demonstrate a knowledge and understanding of scientific ideas, processes, techniques and procedures.

AO2

Apply knowledge and understanding of specific ideas, processes, techniques and procedures:

- in a theoretical context
- in a practical context
- when handling qualitative data
- when handling quantitative data.

Analyse, interpret and evaluate a range of scientific information, ideas and evidence including in relation to issues, to:

- make judgements and reach conclusions

- develop and refine practical design and procedures.

Broadly speaking, **AO1** requires you to tell the examiner what you know. It is, essentially, recalling and stating knowledge that you have gained on your course, and is considered to be the simplest of the three objectives. **AO2** is the trickiest of the three objectives. It requires you to use the knowledge that you have in a new way. These questions are harder to prepare for in advance, as sometimes you have to apply your knowledge to a quote or scenario.

AO3, on the other hand, refers to evaluation. This is about giving the pros and cons of an idea, a piece of research, therapy, theory or explanation. These questions can, theoretically, be prepared for in advance, but if you choose this option, the amount of content you will have to learn to do well in psychology will be enormous! Therefore, the aim of this guide is to help you minimise your rote learning and to improve your skills, so that you can gain higher marks with, theoretically, less knowledge.

ACTIVITY

Draw out 3 spider diagrams: AO1, AO2 and AO3. Then, think about which command words from the lists below would fit into each Assessment Objective (AO).

Evaluate	Explain	Assess	Consider
Describe	State	Apply	Identify
Analyse	Outline	Calculate	Discuss

Thinking point 1: Can you think of any other command words that could be used for any of the AOs?

Thinking point 2: Do any of the words fit into more than 1 AO? If so, would any other words be included?

Thinking point 3: Take a look at a past paper and try to identify which questions belong to which AO, before checking your guesses against the marking scheme.

Skills Builder

CHAPTER 1

AO1 Skills: Knowledge and Understanding

AO1 is considered to be the simplest of the three skills. Once you know what you need to do in each question, in theory, you can learn answers in a more traditional rote learning style. The only problem with this idea is that the amount of knowledge that you would have to 'learn' may feel like a HUGE amount! Therefore, this section of the guide is designed to help you approach the content that you need to learn, in a productive way.

What is AO1?

AO1 requires you to **demonstrate a knowledge and understanding** of scientific ideas, processes, techniques and procedures. This skill is tested on every exam paper, but is most heavily weighed (i.e. there are more marks of this type available) on Unit/Component 1 and 3.

TOP TIP: SPOTTING AO1

AO1 marks are given in questions that use words that have the same meaning as the word 'describe'. Therefore, any time you see words such as outline, state, give an example of, etc. you are being asked to just describe the content in question. Simple right? Well... perhaps not! The way you describe, and the amount of detail required in your description, is also important in AO1. See below for more ideas and examples.

What should I include in an AO1 answer?

⚠ Common Pitfalls

DO NOT include evaluative statements in your AO1 responses. Stating whether something is ethical, reliable, valid, or if it has supporting evidence, are all evaluation points and will not gain you marks in AO1 questions.

Are there any 'rules' you can use to help you work out how much detail to include? Over the next few years, almost all papers will be marked online and will be what examiners call 'constrained' papers (Unit/Component 3 may be an exception to this rule – more on this later on). Constrained papers are those where you will have a question, and then there will be a certain number of lines available for your answer. As a rule of thumb, Psychology exams allow for two lines per mark available. If you have 'average sized handwriting' then this will be enough space, if your writing is very small you may have lines left over, and if your writing is very big you will need extra paper. Extra lines will always be provided at the end of each constrained exam paper. If you use these lines, make sure you label the question you are answering clearly, so that the examiner knows what question you are answering. Below are some examples of real exam questions and student answers that gained a variety of marks.

Outline what is meant by qualitative data. [3] *from WJEC AS Paper, Unit 2, 2017*

This question has 3 marks and would therefore have six lines available. As a general rule in research methods, you need to say something new or add detail to a point you've made, to gain each mark. For this question, you ideally want to outline 3 different things that are associated with qualitative data, or explain two, and then add depth to one of them with an example.

The marking scheme for this question was as follows:

Answers **could** include:

- Descriptive data in the form of words, feelings and emotions.

- In-depth and detailed data.

- Data that in not numerical.

- Data that is produced by methodologies such as a case study or observation.

Student A

Qualitative data is data that contains rich, detailed and descriptive accounts of something and is used when a variable cannot be quantified in numbers. Qualitative data is found in case studies.

The above answer gained 3/3 marks as it was considered a thorough outline of qualitative data. It had at least three key points. One mark was awarded for suggesting that the data is rich in detail, another for the idea that qualitative data is descriptive, and the final mark was awarded to the explanation that the data cannot be quantified in numbers. This candidate actually made a fourth point, by giving an example of when the data would be created (in case studies). You do not lose marks for extra detail, but you should remember that extra time spent on a question that you feel you can answer well, is time you may have wasted by not moving on to another question.

from WJEC AS Paper, Unit 1, 2018

Using an example from psychology, describe the positive assumption of 'authenticity of goodness and excellence'. [4]

To write an effective answer for this question, the description and accuracy of the response must be 'thorough'. So, what does thorough mean? Remember that the question is only worth 4 marks, so thorough in this case does not mean that a long answer is needed. However, you should be aiming to use all of the space available (eight lines) and to relate your response to psychology, by explaining how the assumption links to a human behaviour.

Student B

The assumption of authenticity of goodness and excellence believes that positive emotions such as happiness and goodness are as authentic as negative emotions. Traditional psychological discipline focuses mainly on treating disorders and negative emotions. Seligman (2007) noted that the belief that negative emotions and thoughts are more important than positive ones, has been an obstacle in psychological research.

⚠️ **Common Pitfalls**

DO NOT just repeat the words from the question. Doing this gains no marks at all. Only an explanation/ description of what the terms mean (in this case) will gain credit. Do not use the first line of your answer to write out the question again, as Student B has started to do in their response. Although doing this will make you feel like you have written a longer response, because you will use more lines, this will give you a false sense of security.

This response was considered to be a 'reasonable' description of the assumption. At AS level (WJEC 2018, Unit 1) this answer achieved 3/4 marks as 3 main points have been highlighted: 1) The idea that negative emotions are as 'authentic' as positive ones, 2) the assertion/ suggestion that positive psychology is different to 'traditional' psychology, and 3) a link to psychology through the inclusion of Seligman's view. However, it should be noted that for A level (Eduqas Component 1) this response would be unlikely to gain 3 marks, as the standard expected is higher, due to all the components in the course being at A Level standard, and not AS.

Unfortunately, there are a number of weaknesses in this response – firstly, the description of what 'goodness and excellence' actually are, is lacking. The examples of 'positive emotions' are weak, where happiness and 'goodness' are indicated. Goodness is not an emotion and is just a repetition of wording in the question. In addition, the idea that positive psychology is different to traditional psychology, is only implied – ideally, this should have been made explicit, preferably through an example. For this reason, you can see why the response is not considered to be thorough (4/4 marks), in fact, it is closer to basic

(2/4 marks). It is only because of the inclusion of Seligman's research, as an 'example from psychology', that the student can access 3 marks.

Student B – Improved response

The assumption believes that positive emotions such as happiness, which is made up of feelings such as joy, pride and gratitude, are as authentic as negative emotions. Traditional psychological discipline focuses mainly on treating disorders and negative emotions, however, positive psychology hopes instead to enhance the lives of ALL people, not just those in psychological distress. Seligman (2007) noted that the belief that negative emotions and thoughts are more important than positive ones, has been an obstacle in psychological research. Therefore, he encourages people to participate in activities such as gratitude visits. This will enhance their lives and help to prevent psychological distress before it occurs.

The improved response above is now 'thorough'. This is because it is more comprehensive, it does not repeat ideas, or the question (improving accuracy), and it clearly has four main points to address the question. Improvements can be seen in white, where explicit details about how positive psychology differs from traditional psychology are made. In addition, key terminology from the approach has been integrated, such as the inclusion of 'gratitude visits', to enable the response to gain all the marks on offer.

TOP TIP: GETTING TOP MARKS

Ensure that your answer is both accurate and thorough. To do this, you must not include any irrelevant information and you should elaborate your points with examples and use key terminology. The more scientific your terms (as psychology is considered to be a science), the better!

Assumptions Questions: Unit/Component 1

An example of a common AO1 question on Unit/Component 1 is a 'describe one/two/three assumptions of...' question. Each assumption is most commonly attributed between 3 and 5 marks.

NOTE: *This is not a 'rule', assumptions could be worth more, or less marks each year. This means that you need to know enough information for 5 marks (or more), but you also need to consider what information you should miss out if it is worth only 3 marks. Just learning assumptions off by heart (rote learning) will mean you could waste time on these 'easier' questions and then not have enough time available for more complex questions on the paper.*

TOP TIP: HOW MUCH SHOULD I LEARN?

Don't think of the assumptions as separate pieces of information. In most approaches, the assumptions often complement each other and do not stand alone. For example, in the positive approach, the existence of free will, goodness and excellence, and the good life are all linked, i.e. a person, according to this approach, can use their free will to make choices that achieve goodness and excellence, or the good life. Thinking about how the different assumptions are linked would help you to write more material, if the mark allocation is higher – you do NOT need to learn more 'stuff'. Just use what you already know, in a different way.

from WJEC AS Paper, Unit 1, 2017

Using examples from psychology, describe two assumptions of the biological approach. [4+4]

For this question, your answer for **each** assumption should be roughly eight lines long. This should be enough space to say what the assumption is (one mark), explain it in a couple of sentences (two more marks) and then give an example of how it is used in psychology (perhaps through a study) to elaborate on your point (4 marks!). If you know more about the assumption (which is often more common with the psychodynamic approach), don't just write down everything you know. The key here is your example of behaviour from psychology – the elusive fourth mark. If your assumption is just 'common sense' and not linked to psychology or behaviour, then you cannot gain all the marks on offer, no matter how much you write. It is quality and not quantity that matters.

One way that you could write an effective assumptions answer, is to use the following acronym (PEB). Sticking to this format will prevent you from writing too much detail, but will also allow you to write an effective answer by linking the assumption to a psychological behaviour.

P   Make the **point** – state what the assumption is.

E   **Explain** the core principles of the assumption using technical terms – this will be 2 or 3 sentences about the assumption and what it involves (2 sentences for lower mark allocations – more elaboration for higher marks).

B   Link the assumption to a **behaviour** – explain how one aspect of the assumption could cause a specific type of behaviour e.g. depression, aggression, or relationship formation.

⚠ **Common Pitfalls**

Do not write too much! Lots of students, particularly when writing about the assumptions of the psychodynamic approach, write far too much detail. You need to ensure that all of the core themes and ideas are included, but you should elaborate on them through your examples of behaviour, rather than writing reams and reams of information about every stage of, for example, psychosexual development.

Student A

One assumption of the biological approach is neurotransmitters. These are chemical messengers sent from the brain that travel through the central nervous system and affect our moods. They are: serotonin, adrenaline and dopamine. Too much or too little of a neurotransmitter can affect our moods, for example, too little serotonin can result in depression.

This candidate has made a 'reasonable' attempt to explain one biological assumption (the role of neurotransmitters) and has related it to psychological behaviour, by explaining how serotonin links to depression. This is the P and the B of PEB. However, this candidate only gains 3/4 marks because their explanation (E) is not what would be considered 'thorough', as it lacks the detail needed. It is also slightly repetitive, as it states that neurotransmitters 'affect our mood' (quite a vague statement) twice. An additional sentence to show more detailed psychological understanding, such as an example about the role of SSRIs (anti-depressants) and how they correct chemical imbalances, could perhaps have been enough to gain that final mark.

Student B

The second assumption of the biological approach is neurotransmitters. Neurons are electrically excited cells that form the basis of our nervous system. At the end of these cells are dendrites which branch out and connect neurons with many others – this is where chemical messengers, known as neurotransmitters, are passed on. Neurotransmitters are released from presynaptic vesicles. Neurotransmitters impact our mood and behaviour. For example, the neurotransmitter serotonin has been linked with mental disorders such as depression. Another example is dopamine. Dopamine has been associated with psychotic mental disorders. High levels of dopamine are linked with symptoms of schizophrenia.

The candidate above has gone above and beyond the expectation for 4 marks. They used more than the prerequisite eight lines (they originally used 12 when the response was handwritten), but they have also explained the assumption in a more sophisticated way than Student A. The use of terminology such as 'dendrites' and 'pre-synaptic vesicles' shows a more thorough knowledge that is routed in psychological understanding. Therefore, they gain 4/4 marks. Consequently, finding a balance between the amount you need to write, and the sophistication of your answer, is the key.

Therapies Questions: Unit/Component 1

These questions will ask you to describe/outline/explain one therapy out of a choice of two. For this type of question, you will need to describe the therapy you have learned about in class, using examples where appropriate.

Describe the main components of psychosurgery OR drug therapy. *[12]*

from WJEC AS Paper, Unit 1, 2016

Describe the components of aversion therapy OR systematic desensitisation. *[8]*

from Eduqas AS Paper, Component 1, 2017

For a 'describe the main components of...' question, your answer could be in two parts. Part 1 could include the **aim** of the therapy and the **process/relationship between the client and the therapist**, e.g. what happens when they first attend a session? What do the sessions hope to achieve? This part will be relatively short and perhaps only be a few lines long. Part 2 should make up the bulk of your answer. It should describe the **specific tasks/steps that are completed** during the therapy. There will usually be 3 or 4 steps/aspects that you should **explain in detail, with examples** of when or how they would be used to treat psychological disorders.

The more technical the terminology you use in your therapy answers, the higher the marks awarded will be. Remember, you are aiming for a 'thorough' response that shows both depth and range. AO1 questions on 'describe the therapy' in the past have been worth between 8 and 12 marks, which means that you would have between 10 and 15 minutes to write your response. However, they can be worth ANY number of marks and your response should be tailored to the mark given and therefore the time constraints. Higher marks should contain more detailed examples, lower mark allocations should be more factual, focusing mainly on the tasks/steps involved during the therapy. Again, for example, if the question was worth 10 marks, you are looking at, on average, around one side of A4 in handwriting (20 lines).

Take a look at the paragraph on the next page from a real student response about mindfulness therapy. It has the basic points you would expect to see, but it could be improved to include more technical terminology in order to gain higher marks.

Student A

... A second component of mindfulness is 'meditation and mindful breathing'. Mindfulness originally comes from Buddhism, when it was established to practice self-control, but it is now widely known in the western world. Meditation is usually practiced in a comfortable position, such as sitting, and the patient tries to calm down and concentrate on only one activity; the meditation and the mindful breathing. The patient consciously focuses on their breathing, which helps to avoid focusing on negative thoughts and helps to focus on one activity, rather than getting distracted. It also helps with developing positive thoughts and becoming aware of one's own surroundings...

⚠️ **Common Pitfalls**

Students often just write a description of a therapy that does not contain psychological terms. For example, they talk about changing the way people 'think' in CBT, rather than talking about altering schemas and faulty processing. Alternatively, in aversion therapy, students often forget to point out how the emetic drug/being sick changes the person's behaviour in the long term. They forget to talk about the fact that it is counter conditioning. Make sure that you try to **use core terms from the assumptions of the appropriate approach**.

This answer is just common-sense. It could have been written by any person who knows what meditation and mindful breathing are, and doesn't really contain any psychology, or explain how this part of therapy would help a client overcome emotional distress or anxiety. One way you could consider improving this response, and your own answers, is to include more complex terminology and specific psychological examples within the answer.

You should try to read around the topic and find real life examples of when each therapy has been used to treat specific psychological disorders, or to improve people's lives more generally. Remember, in the case of mindfulness, you don't have to be ill to benefit from the therapy. If you can include findings of psychological studies, about when or how the therapy has been used successfully. This will not only boost your marks, but also help with any evaluation questions that may be asked. In addition, giving examples of when or why a therapy would be used (e.g. to treat which kinds of disorders), can also increase your score. Linking back to the core assumptions of the approach will help here, where you explain the purpose of the activities, in line with the assumptions of the therapist/psychologist who guides the clients through them.

Student A – Improved response

... A second component of mindfulness is 'meditation and mindful breathing'. Mindfulness originally comes from Buddhism, when it was established to practice self-control. The idea that a person can use their own free will to control their own thoughts is central to the aims of MBCT (Mindfulness Based Cognitive Therapy). Meditation is usually practiced in a comfortable position. During meditation the patient consciously focuses on slow, purposeful breathing, which helps to avoid focusing on negative thoughts and helps the client to live in the present moment. It also helps to develop positive thoughts, by teaching the client that they are not defined by their thoughts and emotions. This technique helps to combat 'auto-pilot', where previously people would go through life without taking notice of their actions and environment. Therefore, this aspect of the therapy allows clients to make clearer choices, to feel more in control of their lives, to be calmer and make healthy decisions. This will ultimately help them to find more joy (achieving the good life) by noticing the positive details of our lives and relationships...

In the example above, you can see how repetitive information has been removed and technical information and examples have been added, to make the purpose of mindfulness therapy (in line with the assumptions) clearer. This response would logically, therefore, gain higher marks in the exam. The quality has improved, and although there is slightly more information, all of that information is now relevant. Alternative ways to improve your therapies answers include the addition of core terminology and psychological jargon. Naming a specific type of mindfulness, for example MBCT (Mindfulness Based Cognitive Therapy), rather than talking about the process in a vague way, would also help.

Additionally, focusing on the steps or tasks involved in the therapy will go a long way to improving your responses. In alternative questions/ therapies, examples such as how a client might complete a thought diary during CBT, or how a therapist helps the client to undo the process of dreamwork to reveal the true meaning of the dream (in dream analysis), would be beneficial. Too many students just note down the key features of a therapy without properly explaining them.

Classic Research Questions: Unit/ Component 1

In these questions you are required to describe/outline the methodology, procedures, findings and/or conclusions of a study. You need to learn about five pieces of classic research, one from each of the five approaches.

Approach	Classic Research
Biological	Raine, A., Buchsbaum, M. and LaCasse, L. (1997). *Brain abnormalities in murderers indicated by positron emission tomography.* Biological Psychiatry, volume 42 (issue 6), pages 495–508.
Behaviourist	Watson, J.B. and Rayner, R. (1920). *Conditioned emotional reactions.* Journal of Experimental Psychology, volume 3 (issue 1), pages 1–14.
Cognitive	Loftus, E. and Palmer, J.C. (1974). *Reconstruction of automobile destruction: an example of the interaction between language and memory.* Journal of Verbal Learning and Verbal Behaviour, volume 13, pages 585–589.
Psychodynamic	Bowlby, J. (1944). *Forty-four juvenile thieves: Their characters and home-life.* International Journal of Psychoanalysis, volume 25 (issues 19–52), pages 107–127.
Positive	Myers, D.G. and Diener, E. (1995). *Who is happy?* Psychological Science, volume 6 (issue 1), pages 10–17.

TOP TIP: CLASSIC RESEARCH

AO1 marks are awarded in these questions for accuracy of information. Accuracy is measured against the ORIGINAL study, as published by the psychologist at the time. Any newer or additional information is not considered creditworthy and not all text books report the study accurately. For example, Loftus completed lots of extra research into eye-witness testimony, but it is not relevant in an AO1 classic research question. It could however be useful for the cognitive contemporary debate (see page 87 for more details) or for evaluation (AO3) questions.

You can read the original articles on the WJEC/Eduqas website, or ask your teacher if they have a copy that you could use. http://bit.ly/2KBKM2Z

How much detail you are realistically going to be able to remember will depend on the type of study. For example, no one would expect you to know about all 44 of Bowlby's juvenile thieves (1944) in detail, or to memorise his 60-page original study, however Loftus and Palmer's (1974) research is much more accessible and as such, you would be expected to recall it in much greater accuracy and detail.

So, what do I actually need to know?

For each study, you should be able to describe the **methodology and procedures**. What's the difference? Think of the methodology as the ingredients to make a cake. It lists everything that you need and includes how much of each ingredient to use. This is like the methodology of a study, which includes the number of participants, their gender, occupations, etc. It also includes where the research was held, what equipment was used and using which methodology, e.g. was it an experiment or a case study?

If the methodology is the ingredients list to bake your cake, the procedures are the step-by-step guide to what to do, or how to make it (the recipe!). In each study, this is a detailed account of what happened at each point of the study, in the order that they happened – it should NOT include any findings (something that is trickier to exclude in some studies than others, e.g. Watson and Rayner's research).

In addition to what happened (procedures) you should know the results. Results are considered to be the **findings** of a study. What those findings mean and how they can be used to improve lives (the whole purpose of psychology) are known as **conclusions**. As a general rule, findings tend to have numerical or descriptive data, e.g. the % of people who believed that money was important to future happiness in Myers and Diener's study, or details about the number of thieves in Bowlby's research who had prolonged separations. Conclusions, on the other hand, tend to create new ideas or confirm existing knowledge, based on the findings of the study once it is completed. For example, Loftus and Palmer confirmed in experiment 1 that people are not good judges of speed (in line with past research in this area), and Myers and Diener came up with their own theory of happiness, based on their literature review.

Common Pitfalls

You MUST NOT include details about a part of the study you have not been asked about in these types of questions. For example, when describing the procedures of Watson and Rayner's research with Little Albert, you should not explain when/if he cried, or any of his responses to the loud noises and various objects he was shown. You need to be as accurate as possible for these questions, and any irrelevant information will impact on your accuracy and waste valuable time.

TOP TIP: CLASSIC RESEARCH

Answers to these questions do not have to be written in full sentences. You can use bullet points to list key methodological points and procedures, and you can draw tables of results for the findings.

For more ideas and tips about writing answers to classic research questions, see page 104 of this book in the Questions and Answers section.

Research methods: Including social and developmental psychology

AO1 in research methods papers tends to be very factual and is often allocated low marks, e.g. 1–4 mark questions. The key here is to ensure that you can explain/describe all of the research methods and sampling techniques listed in the specification. You should also be able to define the key psychological terminology associated with the research methods, such as ethical issues and types of reliability and validity. There is a list of the full definitions for all research methods terms (including descriptive and inferential statistics) on the WJEC/Eduqas website:

wjec cbac http://bit.ly/2H65J3H

eduqas http://bit.ly/2N1gdp0

Students often find that making sets of sort cards for the different research methods topics, helps them to learn the definitions and

differences between the key terms. Knowing each term, with an example, will be enough to see you through on these papers – it's tedious, but there really is no other way around it. Putting your knowledge to use in the personal investigations should really help to ground that knowledge. Some examples of research methods AO1 questions can be seen below:

Describe the main features of a case study. [4]

from Eduqas A2 Sample Assessment Materials, Component 2

Define the term 'researcher bias'. [2]

from WJEC AS Paper, Unit 2, 2017

Describe, using examples, the main features of content analysis. [4]

from WJEC AS Paper, Unit 2, 2017

Define what is meant by the term 'operationalisation of variables'. [2]

from WJEC AS Paper, Unit 2, 2017

What's all this about social and developmental psychology?

On Unit/Component 2, you can be asked about social and developmental psychology through two key studies: Milgram's (1963) research into obedience, and Kohlberg's (1968) research into moral development. Milgram is considered to be social psychology, whilst Kohlberg is developmental. You can be asked to discuss the methodology, ethics or any other aspect of research methods – therefore, it is important that you know what they are. This sounds like extra learning, but it isn't, because through your broader studies of psychology you will have covered this. Social psychology concerns research conducted into topics, such as social conformity/ influence (Asch and/or Zimbardo) and obedience (Milgram), whereas developmental psychology concerns research conducted into child development (Kohlberg, Bowlby and, to a lesser extent, Freud). Because you will have studied many of these other psychologists across the different papers (developmental psychology mainly arising in Unit 1 and the mother as a primary caregiver debate, and social psychology through ethics as part of Unit/Component 2) you just need to apply what you already know to this type of question.

Whilst you will not be asked AO1 questions in the same way as Unit/ Component 1 for Milgram and Kohlberg, you do need to know the studies well to answer questions in the exam. Knowledge required is implicit rather than explicit (if you don't know about them, you won't be able to answer questions, but if you do, you won't be able to write an answer you have learned from memory like with the classic research, because the wording that can be used is broader). For classic research on Unit/Component 1, wording generally follows the format of 'describe the (insert term here) of xxx's study into....'. Terms can only be taken from either a single phrase, or a combination of those same phrases: methodology, procedures, findings and/ or conclusions. However, on Unit/Component 2, any phrasing used in the specification for that unit can be utilised, opening up a much broader range of questions. For example:

from Eduqas AS Paper, Component 2, 2016

Describe Milgram's sample and outline how he selected them for his (1963) 'Behavioral Study of Obedience'. [8]

This question requires knowledge (AO1) of Milgram's methodology and participants that is used in a different way. You need to know what happened in Milgram's study (methodology) and how he did it (procedures), but you need to respond specifically with just details about the sample AND how that sample was selected. For example, you may know that he used a volunteer sample of males, but you need to explain how he did this to select his participants, perhaps including details about why he made those decisions. For example, discussing his newspaper advertisement in the Newhaven newspaper and how he selected from those participants who applied to take part.

Other questions might ask you to evaluate either of these two studies (AO3 – see the later section of this book), but you can't do this without having knowledge of what happened (AO1).

from Eduqas AS Paper, Component 2, 2017

Evaluate Kohlberg's (1968) research 'The child as a moral philosopher'. [10]

However, just a word of caution... do not spend a disproportionately long time learning about these studies. Learn them well with a broad brush (get the general gist, focusing mainly on methodology, participants and procedures), and then use your broader psychological knowledge to respond to questions as they arise. Thinking about how and why these two studies were conducted, in the light of both their era (the time in which they were conducted) and purpose (the aims of the study) is much more important than being able to state a number of facts.

NOTE: *for more examples of Milgram and Kohlberg questions, please see page 45 in the AO2 section of this book.*

Maths Skills: Is this really AO1?

Yes and no. You need to know how to complete mathematical calculations and which statistical test is most appropriate for research and why (all knowledge – AO1), but if you are asked to actually calculate some maths, this would be AO2.

Descriptive statistics

So, what do you need to know? You need to know how to calculate or be able to describe how you would calculate: the mean, median, mode, range and standard deviation. All fairly basic GCSE maths until I said 'standard deviation', right?! The standard deviation is the trickiest to calculate and explain, not because the maths is harder, just because it's hard to explain what it is. If you are asked to define the standard deviation, you can use the definition from the WJEC/ Eduqas website (see below). If you are asked why/when it would be used, that's a whole different ball game.

Definition: Standard Deviation (SD)

'A measure that shows the spread of data, whether it is tightly clustered or has a broader spread'.

Data that has a low standard deviation has tightly clustered data that is closer to the mean, data that has a high standard deviation has a broader spread, which implies either a higher number of anomalies, or a skew in the data.

When/why the SD would be used

We look at the standard deviation as a measure of dispersion – how far are most of the scores from the mean? Unlike the range, this measure of dispersion isn't skewed as severely by anomalous data (data that doesn't fit with the rest of the set). If the standard deviation is low, we can assume that most scores are clustered around the mean in a normal distribution (see diagram on the next page) – where 68% of all scores are within one SD (34% above and 34% below the mean). For example, if your mean was 10 and your SD was 5, you could confidently say that 68% of the scores are between 5 and 15. This type of range reduces the impact of anomalies (without ignoring them completely) and gives you a better idea about where the majority of the data falls.

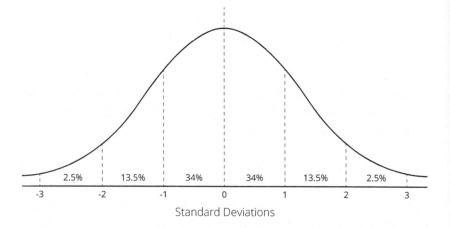

Standard Deviations

Why is this important? Because data that is clustered close to the mean, can be considered more internally valid, as it contains less inconsistences, and the mean can be considered a reliable average of all data in the set. Why do you need to know this? Because if you are asked to evaluate the SD, then you need to be able to compare it to other measures of dispersion. The SD is more sophisticated than the range (which is skewed by anomalies) and it gives us a mathematical measure of all of the data in a normal distribution, rather than just the highest and lowest scores.

Calculating the SD

In the exam, you will be given the formula if you are asked to calculate the SD. But this will be no use to you if you don't KNOW (AO1) what the different symbols in the formula mean.

$$\sqrt{\frac{\sum(x-\bar{x})^2}{n-1}}$$

Looks complicated right? Wrong. There is nothing in this formula that you cannot do, especially when you can use a calculator! So, what do all these symbols mean?

What's this crazy E? ∑ is the symbol for 'the sum of'. In this case, it wants the total (sum) of the calculations on the top line.

 The little x represents the 'score'. So, in this case, it is each separate score in the data set.

 x with a line above it (said x bar) represents the 'mean score', where you take all the scores and divide it by n (see below) to find the average.

2 The little 2 requires you to square your calculation (squaring a number means to multiply the number by itself, e.g. 2^2 is $2 \times 2 = 4$, or 5^2 is $5 \times 5 = 25$).

> ⚠ **Common Pitfalls**
>
> Lots of students work out parts of this calculation in their head, or on a calculator, and don't write down what they did. You lose marks for not showing your workings, if the question asks you to. For example, you might work out the mean on the calculator and write the result on your exam paper, but you don't write down how the mean was calculated, (e.g. what you added together and how many you divided it by) as you just 'did it'! You must write down all parts of the calculation to access all the marks on offer.

$$\sum (x - \overline{x})^2$$

To calculate this top line, the exam board suggests that you can use a table. The first thing you must do is to calculate the mean $\overline{x}$ and place it in the second column – don't forget to show your workings. **= 25+26+21+24 = 96/4 = 24**

Score x	Mean $\overline{x}$	Score minus the mean $(x - \overline{x})$	Score minus the mean squared $(x - \overline{x})^2$
25	24		
26	24		
21	24		
24	24		
	$\sum (x - \overline{x})^2$		

Then, you must complete the calculation in column 3 $(x - \overline{x})$. You do this by subtracting the mean (second column) from the score (first column).

Score x	Mean $\overline{x}$	Score minus the mean $(x - \overline{x})$	Score minus the mean squared $(x - \overline{x})^2$
25	24	1	
26	24	2	
21	24	-3	
24	24	0	
		$\sum (x - \overline{x})^2$	

Then, you complete column 4 $(x - \overline{x})^2$ by simply squaring each number in column 3.

⚠ **Common Pitfalls**

Remember that the negative (-) disappears after being squared.

Score x	Mean $\overline{x}$	Score minus the mean $(x - \overline{x})$	Score minus the mean squared $(x - \overline{x})^2$
25	24	1	1
26	24	2	4
21	24	-3	9
24	24	0	0
		$\sum (x - \overline{x})^2$	

Finally, you total (work out the sum of $\sum$) column 4 to get the score for the top row of the equation.

Score x	Mean $\bar{x}$	Score minus the mean $(x - \bar{x})$	Score minus the mean squared $(x - \bar{x})^2$
25	24	1	1
26	24	2	4
21	24	-3	9
24	24	0	0
		$\sum (x - \bar{x})^2$	**14**

The hardest part is now over. To complete the rest of the calculation, you move to the second row of the equation.

$n - 1$ n is merely the number of scores in the data set. In this case we have 4 scores, so n = 4. To complete this step, you just minus 1 from n, e.g. $n - 1$ **= 4 – 1 = 3**

So far our equation looks like this:

$$\sqrt{\frac{\sum (x - \bar{x})^2}{n - 1}} \qquad \frac{14}{3}$$

We need to complete this division, where the line between the top and bottom row represents 'divide', **14 ÷ 3 = 4.67** (We have rounded to two decimal places, but you should leave the full figure on your calculator).

The final step that will give you the standard deviation, is to calculate the **square root of 4.67**. This is shown in the only symbol of the equation remaining √

$$\sqrt{\frac{\sum (x - x)^2}{n - 1}} = \sqrt{\frac{14}{3}} = \sqrt{4.67} = \text{Thus the SD is 2.16}$$

Inferential Statistics (A Level only)

You will need to be able to select an appropriate statistical test to complete your personal investigations. For this, you need to know when and how they are used. If you memorise a flow chart like this one (see below) in the exam, you will be able to select an appropriate test for unseen data, should you need to (this is an AO2 skill), but you'll also be able to plan your personal investigations better, based on the type of study, the data it creates and your research design.

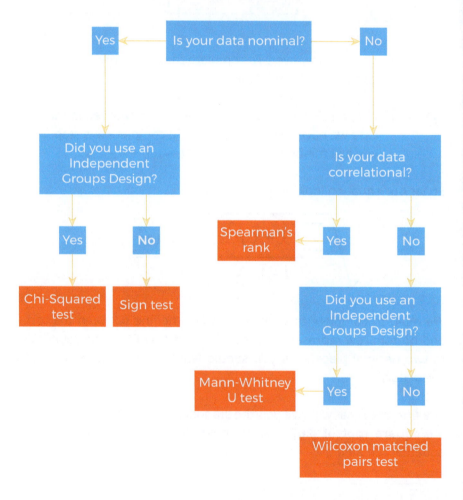

Psychology > Choosing your Statistical Test

http://www.eduqas.co.uk/psychology

Once you know which test to use, how do you know whether your results are significant? This is where the 'R up' rule comes in handy. If there is an R in the short name of the test, like in Chi SquaRe and SpeaRman's Rank, then the observed value (X^2 or Rho) needs to be equal to or higher than the critical value, for results to be considered statistically significant. If there is not an R in the shortened version of the name (all other tests – Sign, Wilcoxon, Mann Whitney), then the rule is reversed, and to be significant, the critical value must be equal to or higher than the observed value (S, T or U). Critical values are taken from pre-calculated tables for each test. For more help on this, you or your teacher can download fact sheets about each statistical test from the 2017–18 training materials link on the WJEC/Eduqas websites:

http://bit.ly/2yW7QCF

http://bit.ly/31wUvwM

AO1 in Unit/Component 3: Implications of psychology in the real world

Unit/Component 3 is taken at the end of two years of psychological study. As such, it is expected that your knowledge and understanding will be at a level that is in line with your experience (2 years, rather than just the 1 year for AS). All straight AO1 questions on this Unit/Component are worth **10 marks** (we will come back to combination questions, where Assessment Objectives are combined, later).

For 10 marks, you will be expected to write somewhere in the region of 20 lines (or more, but certainly not less) – which is approximately 1 side of A4. This Unit/Component is unlikely to be constrained (printed on paper that has lines under each question), because each school or college will complete questions on different topics and you would end up with lots of empty pages. This means that you will have a lined answer booklet for the whole Unit/Component. So you can write as little or as much as you want for each question (you can ask for an extra answer booklet if needed, but remember to label your question clearly).

AO1 questions within Section A of this paper (topics and applications) will focus on knowledge and understanding of: characteristics of the behaviour; biological, individual differences and social psychological explanations of the behaviour in question; two named methods of modification (therapies that aim to reduce/prevent the behaviour in question). You should answer questions on three out of the five available behaviours. For each behaviour, there will be at least two questions, where 10 marks are AO1, 5 are AO2 and 10 are AO3 (we will return to these other questions later).

Characteristics of behaviour

AO1 questions on characteristics of behaviour can look like the following examples from past Units/Components:

from WJEC A2 Sample Assessment Materials, Unit 3	*Describe the characteristics of schizophrenia.* [10]
from Eduqas A level paper, Component 3, 2018	*Outline the characteristics of bullying behaviours.* [10]
from WJEC A2 paper, Unit 3, 2017	*Describe the characteristics of autistic spectrum behaviours.* [10]

Describe the characteristics of behaviours that lead to a diagnosis of schizophrenia. [10]

from Eduqas A level Sample Assessment Materials, Component 3

This type of question can come up for any behaviour, in addition to those above, e.g. criminal behaviour, addictive behaviour, stress, bullying and so on. This is perhaps an easier type of question within the topics section as you could, in theory, prepare and learn an answer in advance of the exam. As you will only revise three different topics, the workload to do this is not particularly onerous. However, it is important to note that the wording of the question, even within the same topic, could alter slightly and you should tailor your response to address this. An example of this can be seen above, where two of the four questions are on characteristics of schizophrenia. Both these questions effectively require the same knowledge, but the last of the four questions would read better, (and is therefore more likely to get higher marks) if the response used phrasing such as 'one characteristic that a psychologist/psychiatrist might look for when diagnosing schizophrenia is....'. This slight alteration in the language is likely to push a good response into the upper band (thorough knowledge), rather than the material being considered to be reasonable (where there is nothing wrong with the response, but it just doesn't fully address the question based on the way it is worded).

In a 'characteristics' question, it is recommended that you first briefly **define the behaviour being discussed**. What is it? For example, for behaviours that are listed in the DSM (Diagnostic Statistical Manual), like Addiction, Schizophrenia and Autism, you could consider describing the generic psychological or physical symptoms and changes in the body associated with that behaviour. For the behaviours not listed, like crime, bullying and stress, you should try to define them in terms of actions/behaviours that are typical.

Next, you could subdivide your response into two or more paragraphs to structure your response. You might first want to **discuss how the behaviour is regarded by society or diagnosed by a psychologist**. For example, stress is considered to be a natural bodily response and as such, is not always negative, whereas criminal behaviour is considered to be immoral at different levels. Here, you could discuss the behaviour in question, with specific examples of bodily processes/symptoms of the behaviour. Information that would fit into this paragraph or section of your answer can be found in traditional textbooks and this is a good starting point for your response.

However, if you want your response to stand out, and to go that one step further (possibly allowing you to access the highest mark band), a final paragraph would be beneficial. This should focus on **unique features of people who participate in the behaviour** in question. For example, what makes an autistic person different to someone without autism? Or, what is the difference between criminal behaviours and non-criminal behaviours? Are some people more prone to addictive behaviour than others? This discussion can pull knowledge from your explanations of behaviour. For example, you could include information in a response about addiction from Eysenck's psychological resource model of personality, by explaining that people who have certain traits (such as psychoticism) are more likely to become addicts. Alternatively, you could discuss the characteristics of different types of criminals, such as organised and disorganised killers.

Explanations of behaviour

For each behaviour, you need to be able to describe six different explanations for that behaviour. Two of each from biological, individual differences and social psychological explanations. How much do you need to know about each explanation? It is always useful to know both explanations from each subsection (biological, individual differences and social psychological) well enough for a 10 mark question. This is most likely what your teachers will provide you with. It is then up to you to choose which of the two explanations you feel you understand the most and wish to describe in enough detail for a 10 mark response, to a question such as those listed below.

from Eduqas A2 Paper, Component 3, 2018

Describe one social psychological explanation of criminal behaviour.

[10]

from Eduqas A2 Paper, Component 3, 2017

Describe one social psychological explanation for addictive behaviours.

[10]

What you need to think about here, is how much you can realistically write in the time available. You may 'know' enough to write a 20 mark essay, but you need to learn to be concise in your descriptions of two explanations, so that each one has enough detail, but is not so long that you run out of time for other questions. In other psychology Units/Components, like Unit/Component 1 and 2, you are given two lines per mark. Using this same rule, you should be able to write 5 marks worth of a description within approximately 10 lines or half a side of A4. To do this you would need to be accurate and concise, but it is possible, and it should be something that you aim towards to ensure you do not run out of time on this Unit/Component. That said, this will be very difficult to achieve when writing an A Level (A2) response and so if you need to write more, and you have enough time, you should do so. This paper is unconstrained (you will not be provided with a set number of lines), so it is important that you keep track of the time during the exam, so that you do not get carried away and run out of time to complete other questions.

Describe two biological explanations for stress. [10]

Describe two social psychological explanations of addictive behaviours. [10]

Describe two explanations of autistic spectrum behaviours. [10]

(a) (i) Describe one biological explanation for criminal behaviours. [5]

(ii) Describe one individual differences explanation for criminal behaviours. [5]

Describe two individual differences explanations of schizophrenia. [5+5]

Remember to be careful with your time. You can see some good examples in the Q&A section of this book on page 107. I have seen students write up to four pages in exams on one question before, and then they run out of time for the other questions.

As a general rule, try to learn a response that will describe the explanation in question for 3/4 marks. Your description should include as much key terminology as possible, making direct links to how the explanation applied to the behaviour in hand. You can then use psychological research studies to add to your explanation. Findings from studies that help to give further detail about the explanation are creditworthy as AO1.

By using knowledge that you might usually use as evaluation (like supporting studies), you can cut down some of your learning, as the same information can be used in different ways – as either AO1 or AO3 – just by changing the wording of your statements.

⚠ Common Pitfalls

When writing a response for an AO1 description of an explanation of a behaviour, you should try to avoid using evaluative terminology,

from Eduqas A2 Paper, Component 3, 2018

from WJEC A2 Paper, Unit 3, 2018

from WJEC A2 Paper, Unit 3, 2018

from WJEC A2 Paper, Unit 3, 2018

from WJEC A2 Paper, Unit 3, 2018

e.g. 'One psychologist who SUPPORTS this theory is...'

Instead, you should try to use descriptive language/terms so that your supporting studies can gain you extra AO1 marks, e.g. 'A psychologist who demonstrated this was....'

Do I need a conclusion in an AO1 question?

In a word... no! If a question is purely a description, there is no quote, and the question is not a combined assessment objective (AO) question, then there is no need for a conclusion. Conclusions are only sometimes necessary in AO1 combination questions, where some of the marks are awarded as AO2 or AO3. See page 89 for more details about how to respond to combination questions with conclusions.

Taking your knowledge (AO1) beyond the textbook

One way that you could expand your knowledge beyond that reported in traditional textbooks, is to gain a deeper understanding of psychological research by completing extra reading. This does not have to be hard work and you can use the basic knowledge that traditional textbooks provide as a starting point.

Internet research and use of videos to enhance learning

One thing that you can do, which is quite portable (you could do this whilst you are on the bus, for example, as you don't need to have all your notes with you), is to complete additional research into your psychological studies. Although this sounds like it could be time consuming, the exam board have made this quite easy for you to do, as they create a monthly document with links to psychological research that has been collated by teachers. In addition, the links document also contains short videos and longer documentaries which you can watch, to learn in a different style.

http://bit.ly/2ma7t4b

http://bit.ly/2l1kQ6L

Whilst you are reading articles or watching videos, you should try to solidify what you are doing, so that the activity becomes active rather than passive. How often have you watched a whole episode of a programme and then barely been able to remember what happened afterwards? You don't want this to happen if the purpose is learning, and therefore whilst you are reading/watching, you could complete a little list/summary, using the following prompts (known as a reflection frame).

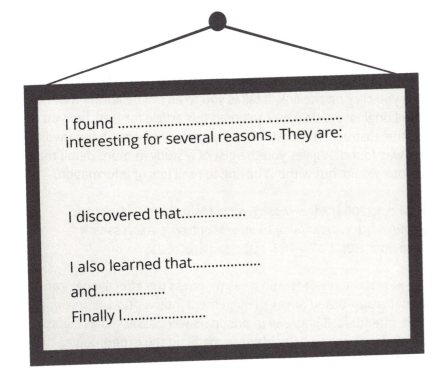

I found .... interesting for several reasons. They are:

I discovered that..................

I also learned that..................
and..................
Finally I......................

You can access two online learning frames here:
http://bit.ly/2OVUcdM

Reading abstracts

Textbooks will usually sum up what a psychologist found, said or did in a single sentence. This means that you often know very little about that piece of research and this would make it more difficult to evaluate. In order to gain a better understanding, but without having to read lots of research, you could look up the abstract for that study.

For example, a commonly quoted piece of psychological research is that of David and Avellino (2002). They suggest that CBT is the most successful of all therapies. Well that's what other textbooks and online sources will tell you... But it is fair to say that this snippet is pretty much all a student knows about their work. We don't know how they came to this conclusion, or how many other therapies were considered. To find out more, you could read the abstract of David and Avellino's work or do an internet search on websites such as google scholar.

Whilst original journal articles in full are usually paid for, you can read the abstract of almost any piece of research for free. Another example of a piece of research, that is commonly quoted to highlight the effectiveness of anger management as a technique to reduce crime, is Ireland's (2004) work. If we use a website like google scholar to search for 'Ireland 2004 anger management', his original article will come up. When you click on the link, it takes you to an online library that holds the full original article. You can't read this article for free, but you can read the abstract. The abstract is a summary of what happened and what was found. It gives you the gist of a study in more detail than a textbook would, but without having to read lots of information.

Ireland, J. (2004) *Anger management therapy with young male offenders: An evaluation of treatment outcome.* Aggressive Behaviour, 30(2), 174–185. http://bit.ly/2OV4N8w

The aim of the present study was to assess the effectiveness of a brief group-based anger management intervention with young male offenders. Eighty-seven prisoners were assessed as suitable for the intervention. Fifty of these made up the experimental group and 37 the control. Prior to intervention prisoners completed a self-report anger questionnaire (Anger Management Assessment questionnaire: AMA). Prisoners were also assessed by officers on a checklist addressing angry behaviour (Wing Behaviour Checklist: WBC). Both measures were completed approximately two weeks before the date of the intervention and eight weeks after the intervention (and while the control group remained on the waiting list). It was predicted that the experimental group would show significant improvements in both measures following intervention and that no such change would be observed in the control group. This hypothesis was supported, with significant improvements observed in the experimental group and no change observed in the control.

Once you have the abstract, (as above), you could make some brief notes using the following format:

- Name of main researcher(s):

- Date:

- What did they do?

- What did they find?

- Does this support or refute the effectiveness of ....?

Using this technique will enable you to not only better understand the study you are describing, but it will allow you to make counterarguments that comment on the validity of the study in light of the methodology, etc. This could be particularly helpful if you have a 10 mark evaluation question, but only know a limited number of studies to support/refute the effectiveness of anger management.

CHAPTER 2

AO2 Skills: Application of knowledge

A lot of students find AO2 to be one of the most difficult skills to master in A level Psychology, but once you know how to spot AO2 exam questions, you should be able to easily adapt your existing knowledge and skills to gain higher marks.

What is AO2?

AO2 requires you to **apply your knowledge and understanding** of scientific ideas, processes, techniques and procedures. This could be in a theoretical context in Unit/Component 1 and 3, or in a practical context when handling qualitative and quantitative data, in research methods papers.

> ✏️ **TOP TIP: SPOTTING AO2**
>
> AO2 marks are given in questions that use words that have the same meaning as the word 'apply', that have a quote or scenario, or that ask you to explain an idea in context. For example, questions that are related to Milgram and/or Kohlberg in Unit/Component 2.

What should I include in an AO2 answer?

As a general rule of thumb, if you **answer the question in front of you**, you will get the marks available. This might sound obvious, but lots of students get carried away in the exam and give an answer they have learned 'off by heart' that does not answer the question they were given.

AO2 may contain knowledge and understanding that has been used (applied) in a new way. For example, the AS level question below (from the SAMS – Sample Assessment Materials) requires you to apply your knowledge about the assumptions to a specific behaviour, in this case to relationship formation.

from Eduqas AS Sample Assessment Materials, Component 1

Describe how one assumption from the positive approach can be applied to relationship formation.
[4]

For this question you shouldn't just describe one of the assumptions of the positive approach. Doing this will gain a score of 0/4 as the marks are allocated as AO2, which means you must explain **how** the assumption is '**applied** to relationship formation' to gain any credit. An example of an exam question that fits into this theme (applying assumptions to relationship formation), with real student answers and examiner comments, can be seen in the second half of this guide on page 107.

Do I need a conclusion in an AO2 question?

If a question is worth 10 marks or more, you should always consider whether your answer requires a conclusion. Conclusions are not required for simple AO1 questions, but they are always required for AO3 when the allocation of marks is 10 or more. Some AO2 questions do need a conclusion, others do not. It really depends on the question.

Below are some examples of AO2 questions from past exam papers. Questions 1 and 2 DO NOT require a conclusion as they are either worth fewer than 10 marks (question 1), or they require you to apply knowledge (both question 1 and 2). Application of knowledge, like in AO1, does not need a conclusion, regardless of the number of marks.

1. *Explain why a psychologist following the biological approach would consider drug therapy OR psychosurgery as a suitable therapy.* [5]

from Eduqas AS Paper, Component 1, 2016

2. *'By asking who is happy, and why, we can help people rethink their priorities and better understand how to build a world that enhances human well-being'.*
(Myers and Diener, 1995)
With reference to the above quote and using your own knowledge, explain how the positive approach could be applied to human behaviour in practical contexts. [12]

from Eduqas A2 Sample Assessment Materials, Component 1

The following questions, however, DO require a conclusion as the question requests applied evaluation. The rule is that any evaluation question that is worth 10 marks or more requires a conclusion (see AO3 skills for more details), this is still true even when the evaluation is applied (AO2).

3. *'Biological therapies are successful in treating mental illness.' With reference to the above statement, discuss the effectiveness of either drug therapy or psychosurgery, using psychological knowledge and research.* [10]

from Eduqas A2 Paper, Component 1, 2017

from WJEC AS Paper, Unit 1, 2016

"The biological approach may be more scientific than the psychodynamic approach. However, the psychodynamic approach still has some advantages over the biological approach." With reference to the above statement, compare and contrast the biological and psychodynamic approaches in terms of their similarities and differences. [10]

All command words associated with evaluation (see page 59 of this guide) that are allocated 10 marks or more will require a conclusion. This rule applies to all Psychology Units/Components.

How does this information fit in with the different exam Units/Components?

AO2 is assessed in all exam papers. In Unit/Component 1 and research methods papers, each question has separate skills. This means that a question will be either AO1, AO2 or AO3. The only exception to this rule is for Contemporary Debates essays where half of the marks are allocated to AO1 and half are AO3 (see page 86). **Look for command or linking words associated with the term 'apply' to spot AO2** (see page vii of this guide).

In Unit/Component 3, AO2 is sometimes combined with another assessment objective (see page 91 of this guide for specific examples of how to approach AO2 on this Unit/Component).

AO2 on Unit/Component 1: Psychology Past to Present

There are really only two AO2 question types on this Unit/Component. Apply the assumptions questions, and quote/statement questions. AO2 is well worth practicing, because it is usually these questions that are the differentiators – they essentially can make the difference between grades. Doing well in AO2 is therefore an important skill to master.

Applying the assumptions of the approach

One part of the specification that is most relevant here is the requirement to 'know and understand how the approach can be used in therapy'. This type of question requires you to explain how the assumptions of the approach are applied, through the main ideology and components of the therapy. Past questions that require you to apply the assumptions to a therapy are as follows:

Explain why a psychologist following the biological approach would consider drug therapy OR psychosurgery as a suitable therapy. **[5]**

from Eduqas AS Paper, Component 1, 2016

Explain why a psychologist from the positive approach would view mindfulness OR quality of life therapy as an appropriate therapy. **[5]**

from WJEC AS Paper, Unit 1, 2017

A psychologist needs to explain to his client why they may be better using a therapy from a biological approach rather than from the cognitive approach. Using your knowledge of both approaches, compare and contrast the cognitive and biological approaches and their therapies. **[10]**

from WJEC AS Sample Assessment Materials, Unit 1

The first two of these questions are quite straight forward. You have to explain why a psychologist might consider the therapy to be appropriate by linking back to the assumptions. But what students often do is just describe the main components of the therapy, instead of justifying why it should/would be used by a psychologist from that particular approach. The answer starts well and is focused on the question, but then gradually wanders off the topic. What you need to do is create a structure to your response, so that you don't just describe the therapy. One way that you can do this is by using the following format:

N — What are the causes of **normal** behaviour according to the assumption(s) of the approach?

A — What causes the types of **abnormal** behaviours that would need to be treated with a therapy? (Use examples.)

A — How would the therapy **aim** to make the abnormal behaviour 'normal' again?

N — How would the processes involved in the therapy (components) create this **normal** behaviour?

You can use the NAAN structure in one of two ways: For longer questions, you could do mini NAAN paragraphs – perhaps one for each assumption of the approach; but for lower mark answers you could just combine the assumptions to use the NAAN structure for your entire answer (where each paragraph is made up of one letter from NAAN).

For example, if we take the top exam question from the list on the previous page (worth 5 marks) and apply the biological assumptions to EITHER drug therapy or psychosurgery, we could use NAAN to structure our whole answer.

TOP TIP: FOCUSING YOUR RESPONSES

In lower mark questions, make sure you focus your response and do not include irrelevant information. For example, in the plans on the next page you will see that the most relevant assumption (applied to the therapy) is the main/first focus of the response. Do not spend too much time writing about less relevant assumptions.

from Eduqas AS Paper, Component 1, 2016

Explain why a psychologist following the biological approach would consider drug therapy OR psychosurgery as a suitable therapy. [5]

PLAN	Drug Therapy	Psychosurgery
N – normal	Balanced neurotransmitters; all localities of the brain working together in harmony; creates evolved prosocial behaviours.	Functions of all localities of the brain are intact and working together; allows for a balance of neural activity and transmission; creates evolved prosocial behaviours.
A – abnormal	Imbalance of neurotransmitters such as serotonin (low levels lead to depression) and dopamine (high levels lead to schizophrenia).	Specific localities of the brain are malfunctioning. For example physical symptoms such as tremors originate in the motor area of the frontal cortex, whereas schizophrenics are found to have irregularities in the corpus callosum.
A – aim	Medical model = drugs to rebalance neurotransmitters.	Medical model = psychosurgery to remove or alter brain irregularities.
N – normal	Use of SSRIs. Use of antipsychotics.	Use of bilateral-cingulotomies (less common). Use of DBS.

NOTE: *A real student answer to this question can be seen in the second section of this book (Questions and Answers) on page 115.*

Using this plan will give you a basic outline, which can then be expanded (in the first A – causes of abnormality, and the second N – aspect of therapy that tackles the problem) for higher mark allocations. Depth and detail will need to be added, through the use of core terminology and specific examples of behaviours that are more commonly treated with the therapy, in order to gain all the marks on offer. You should keep referring back to the question, to ensure that you do not go off topic.

NOTE: *With Eduqas you can also be asked to apply the assumptions to a range of behaviours – see page 111 in the second half of this guide for more details.*

Common Pitfalls

Students will often see a topic or theme within a question, without reading it carefully. Do not be tempted to just write an answer you have learned if it does not fit the question being asked. For example, do NOT describe the therapy if it doesn't ask you to describe it. In this case, we want to know why the therapy is 'suitable', not what it entails.

When writing a response for AO2, try to focus your response to the question. If there is a quote, refer to it, if there isn't, use the wording from the question to frame your response and ensure that you don't go off topic.

Take it further

One way you could expand your response, if there is a higher mark allocation for this type of question, is to briefly justify the choice of therapy by comparing it to another from an alternative approach. For example, you could comment (at the end of your response or within the main body) on why a 'psychologist from the biological approach' would NOT use a therapy such as CBT or dream analysis. This will help to ground your response to the core assumptions of the biological approach and show a deeper understanding. For example:

'A biological psychologist would not treat depression with CBT as they believe that the cause of depression is physical rather than psychological. Instead, by focusing on drug therapy/psychosurgery, as part of a medical model of treatment, they aim to...'

Quote/statement questions

Be aware that some questions with a quote or a statement need to be answered using an AO3 format/style. They will usually be in the form of applied evaluation. Some examples of this type of question can be seen below:

from WJEC AS Paper, Unit 1, 2016

'The biological approach may be more scientific than the psychodynamic approach. However, the psychodynamic approach still has some advantages over the biological approach.'
With reference to the above statement, compare and contrast the biological and psychodynamic approaches in terms of their similarities and differences.

[10]

A teacher was asked which one was the best approach: biological or psychodynamic. Using your knowledge, prepare the teacher's answer by comparing and contrasting the biological and psychodynamic approaches. [10]

from Eduqas AS Paper, Component 1, 2017

A psychologist needs to explain to his client why they may be better using a therapy from a biological approach rather than from the cognitive approach. Using your knowledge of both approaches compare and contrast the cognitive and biological approaches and their therapies. [10]

from WJEC AS Sample Assessment Materials, Unit 1

'Biological therapies are successful in treating mental illness.' With reference to the above statement, discuss the effectiveness of the biological therapy you described in part (a), using psychological knowledge and research. [10]

from Eduqas A2 Paper, Component 1, 2017

All of these questions are applied AO3 (the next section of this book discusses how to write an AO3 response). The first three of these questions are compare and contrast style questions, where your comparisons should be linked back to the statement/quote (examples of student answers with this type of applied evaluation can be seen in the second half of this guide). The final question is a more traditional evaluation question where you would need to use a sandwich structure to frame your paragraph (see page 61). The main thing to remember here is that in each paragraph, you should try to add in a link to the statement or phrase... your response will not be dramatically different to an AO3 response, it just differs as it has links to the statement at the beginning and at the end of the paragraph.

An exam question that allows us to demonstrate this idea is as follows:

A psychology student suggests to his teacher that one of the problems with the behaviourist approach is that it is too simplistic. Explain why this might be considered a strength OR a weakness of the behaviourist approach. [5]

from WJEC AS Paper, Unit 1, 2017

This question is AO2, as you are explaining why a statement is one thing or another. It is important to note here that this question is not a trick – an approach being too simplistic could be considered either a strength or a weakness for equal credit. However, when you frame your answer you should bear in mind that examiners are looking for relevant information that is accurate and thorough, in addition to well-chosen examples from the approach. In the two examples below, you can see links to the statement highlighted in white. These are the aspects that ensure the answer is AO2, as they link directly back to the question stem.

Response as a strength

◊ The psychology teacher could suggest that it is not always 'a problem' for an approach to be 'simplistic'. By taking a simplified approach to explaining behaviour, a strength could be that potential treatments can be sought on the basis of the approach. The behaviourist approach only considers the nurture side of the nature vs nurture debate. Behaviourists suggest that humans and animals learn in similar ways which, although simple, can help us to understand that the causes of behaviour are environmental, as we are all born as a blank slate. In theory, this means that all behaviours are learned through conditioning, even undesirable behaviours like extreme phobias or addictions. By the same token, Behaviourists suggest that undesirable behaviours can be unlearned through treatments that counter-condition clients, such as aversion therapy or systematic desensitisation. By backing up his claims in this way, the teacher can justify to the student that being 'too simplistic' is a strength rather than a weakness of the behaviourist approach.

Response as a weakness

◊ The psychology student could suggest that 'a problem', therefore a weakness of the behaviourist approach, is that it is too simplistic. He should explain that this is a weakness because the approach fails to recognise important differences between human and non-human animals. When behaviourists suggest that a human learns complex behaviours, such as addiction, in the same way as a rat or a pigeon, as part of conditioning, it reduces the complexities of human cognition down to stimulus-response associations. This is reductionist, as factors such as genetics are completely ignored, focusing only on conditioning and observational processes as sources of learning for all behaviours. Furthermore, taking a blank slate approach ignores evolutionary processes that set humans apart from other animals. By backing up his claims in this way, the student will be able to justify that being 'too simplistic' is a weakness rather than a strength of the behaviourist approach.

Both of these responses are perfectly adequate for 5 marks, however if there were a higher mark allocation, or if you are a particularly fast writer, you could add in an example of a psychological study from the approach to back up your points. HOWEVER, do not get carried away – you will only have approximately 6/7 minutes to answer a 5 mark question, so do not spend too much time on this response. The fact that you will only have 10 lines means that, unless you have lots of extra paper, you will not have room or time for this type of expansion.

Take it further

In the first response (as a strength) you could include psychological research about the relative success rates of a behaviourist therapy, whereas in the second (as a weakness) you could expand the response to include an example of a specific behaviour (like addiction or schizophrenia), that is better described by explanations other than conditioning, to justify your response.

These additional points should be brief and no more than one or two additional sentences.

AO2 on Research Methods papers

The majority of the marks on research methods papers are allocated to AO2. Anything relating to how research is conducted, relating to 1) Milgram and Kohlberg, 2) your personal investigations, or 3) a scenario, is considered to be AO2 – applied knowledge. Here you are using what you know, in a new and different way. These types of questions cannot be prepared for in advance and you would be wise to get hold of as many past papers as possible, therefore, to practice these questions.

TOP TIP: ACCESSING PAST PAPERS

One big advantage of studying WJEC or Eduqas Psychology is that there are different papers written for students in England and Wales. Why is this an advantage? Because you can use both sets of papers as practice for your revision. There are a few minor differences. For example, in England there are two sets of Component 1 and 2 in each year (one is AS, and one is A level). A level Component 2 in England combines knowledge from Units 2 and 4 in Wales because it is sat in year 2, not year 1. In addition, the contemporary debates are on Component 1 in England, but on Unit 2 in Wales. Otherwise... everything else is pretty much the same! To access past papers, you can visit BOTH the WJEC (Wales papers) and Eduqas (England papers) websites:

WJEC:
http://bit.ly/2YYZ9SL

Eduqas:
http://bit.ly/2Z2mKpD

NOTE: *the most recent past papers (from the last academic year) can only be accessed by your teacher on the secure website up until March – ask them if they can download it for you for additional practice.*

1. Questions on Milgram and Kohlberg

The purpose of Milgram and Kohlberg questions is to check your understanding of how a piece of research is designed and conducted. To answer these sorts of questions, you will need to be familiar with the work of both psychologists. Your focus of revision should be on the processes involved in the research, rather than on the findings and conclusions. Questions in the exam can be drawn from any part of the specification as listed in Unit/Component 2. This means that questions will centre around the following headings: Deciding on a research question, methodologies, location of research, participants (including sampling), experimental design, levels of measurement, graphical representation, descriptive statistics, inferential statistics (A Level Eduqas/Unit 4 WJEC) reliability, validity and ethics.

Additionally, you may be asked questions that require you to think about what 'could' have happened as part of the research process (some examples can be seen below). If this is the case, you should apply your psychological understanding and knowledge of either Milgram or Kohlberg to what you have learned. Why do psychologists design their research in the way that they do? You can't possibly be expected to know what Milgram or Kohlberg were thinking, but you should be able to understand why they might have made the choices that they did and discuss the implications of those decisions.

Explain one reason why Kohlberg may have chosen only to sample boys from early adolescence onwards, rather than girls, in his research 'The child as a moral philosopher' (1968). [3]

from WJEC AS Paper, Unit 2, 2017

This question asks you to use your psychological imagination to justify why Kohlberg 'may have chosen' only male participants – there is no right or wrong answer, you just need to think about why this might have occurred and justify your response in context (with reference to the psychologist's research). A top band, real life student response can be seen overleaf.

Student A

Kohlberg decided to use only boys for his research as boys mature slightly later than girls. There is a bigger jump with boys' moral reasoning within their adolescent years, so he could clearly see how their moral reasoning changes throughout their childhood. Girls have quite a high moral reasoning from an early age, so he wouldn't be able to see much of a difference.

Examiner comments: Suggestion of Kohlberg's 'choice' (being able to measure differences in development more easily) is detailed and thorough. This is explained through the differing development of males/females. Links to moral reasoning are also present allowing access to the top band. **3/4 marks.**

⚠ **Common Pitfalls**

Relevant examples from the study in question allow you to access higher marks. You will NOT achieve higher marks if the only link to the research is using the psychologist's name. Just writing 'An advantage of self-selected sampling in Milgram's research...' then talking about a generic advantage will not allow you to access all the marks on offer.

The next three questions ask you to explain the impact of the choices these psychologists made on their research and its applications. These are all in a style of applied evaluation and require you to consider potential strengths and weaknesses related to the context/question stem.

from WJEC AS Paper, Unit 2, 2018

In Milgram's (1963) 'Behavioral study of Obedience' he chose to use a target population of male participants. Explain how his choice has impacted on the possible applications of the research. [5]

from WJEC AS Paper, Unit 2, 2017

Milgram's (1963) 'Behavioral study of Obedience' used a volunteer (self-selected) sample.
(a) Describe one advantage and one disadvantage of the use of self-selected sampling in Milgram's study. [4]

from WJEC AS Paper, Unit 2, 2017

As part of his research, 'The child as a moral philosopher' (1968), Kohlberg had to disregard 'culture bound moral concepts.'
(b) Explain how researcher bias might impact the validity of a study, with reference to Kohlberg's research. [6]

Adding details from the research (known as contextualisation) will gain higher marks. For example, 'An advantage of using the New Haven newspaper to select his participants is that Milgram was able to/had...'

Two of these questions focus on the participants involved in Milgram's research, whereas the third concentrates on researcher bias and validity in Kohlberg's research. By understanding these key terms and applying your ideas through examples from the named study, you will be able to access higher bands. If you fail to include relevant examples, your score will be limited to the lower mark bands.

2. Your personal investigations

The thing to remember about your personal investigations is that they are 'personal' to you. The only thing that may be the same between your research and another student's from another school/college, or in a different part of the country is the topic/research title. Each year there are two new titles for the personal investigations:

Assessment Year	Investigation one	Investigation two
Summer 2019	An experiment on the Chameleon effect.	A questionnaire on relationships.
Summer 2020	An experiment on noise and performance.	A content analysis on gender and advertising.
Summer 2021	A questionnaire study of perceived wellbeing after exercise.	A correlational study of time spent revising and scores on a test.

Because the research is open to interpretation and you can design it any way you wish (within reason, as you must use the method identified in the title) the exam questions you will be asked about them have to be relatively generic. Question setters don't know what sampling technique you used, they don't know your research design in an experiment and they don't know the specific variable you chose to 'measure' performance, wellbeing, etc. With this in mind you need to make sure that when you answer questions about your investigations you explain them in explicit detail, stating what you did, how and why you did it. Unlike any other exam question there is no implicit understanding – in another question where, for example, the sampling technique is named, the examiner already has a good idea of what the answer should look like. This is NOT the case in personal investigations as everyone's answer could be different.

Identify two ethical issues you considered when planning your observation and explain how these were dealt with. [3+3]

from WJEC A2 Paper, Unit 4, 2018

The above question demonstrates what we mean here. Because the examiner has no idea how you carried out your observation, in terms of the procedures you undertook, it is impossible for them to know how you will answer this question. The examiner might have a list of potential ethical issues in mind that you should have considered before completing your study, such as valid consent, risks to participants, confidentiality and so on, but they don't know how you tackled them. For this reason, you should ensure that you explain, in detail, exactly what happened during the planning of your research and what procedures you set in motion in order to ensure that they were dealt with appropriately. All the way through your response you should refer back to your own research with examples – you don't want your response to be 'floaty'. See page 71 for details of how to avoid this pitfall and to ensure all responses are 'sticky'.

ACTIVITY

Let's, for the sake of argument, say that you got this exact same question for one of your own personal investigations: Identify two ethical issues you considered when planning your (insert research method here) and explain how these were dealt with. [3+3]

Take the sentence starters below and write an answer for your own personal investigation. Remember, you MUST use examples from your own investigation and relate back to the title (known as contextualisation).

One ethical issue I considered when planning my research into .... was valid consent. To ensure that I gained consent that was valid I .... (INSERT YOUR DETAILS HERE WITH EXAMPLES) .... In addition, I also decided not to include any participants under the age of 16 as the BPS suggests that for consent to be valid I would need both the participants' permission to ... (INSERT TASK TO BE UNDERTAKEN HERE) ... and the permission of their parent/guardian.

Another ethical issue that I had to deal with when .... was confidentiality. To maintain confidentiality of .... (INSERT TARGET POPULATION HERE) ... I did not request any personal information that was not pertinent to the investigation into .... The only information I recorded about the participants was details about .... (INSERT YOUR DETAILS HERE

WITH EXAMPLES) .... This ensured that any risks to participants if their data was to be seen by third parties would have been minimised.

A common area that students struggle with in research methods generally, but also in the personal investigations, is operationalisation of variables. To operationalise a variable means to define and/or measure it. Past questions on this include:

Explain how you operationalised sharing behaviour in your observation. [2]

from WJEC A2 Paper, Unit 4, 2018

Explain how the dependent variable was operationalised. [2]

from WJEC A2 Paper, Unit 4, 2017

Identify the fully operationalised co-variable in your research other than intelligence. [2]

from Eduqas A2 Paper, Component 2, 2018

State the operationalised co-variables that you used in your correlational research. [2]

from Eduqas A2 Paper, Component 2, 2017

Whilst all these questions occurred in different years or in different countries (Wales and England), you can see a general theme to the questions. You get (roughly) one mark for picking out what the variable actually was and the other for saying how it was specifically measured or defined. When operationalising, you should include the unit of measurement that you used within the research. For example, for the 2020 experiment into noise and performance you will need to define what is meant by the term 'noise' and outline how you measured 'performance'. You could do this in MANY ways, and there is no correct response, but you need to make sure that you are clear about what 'noise' or 'performance' actually mean in your investigation. Does 'noise' mean that in one condition there was silence and in the other there was classical music being played? OR does it mean that in one condition there was quiet music at 20 decibels and in the other there was loud music at 90 decibels? It really doesn't matter what you choose, but you should be able to explain it in the exam. Additionally, how was 'performance' measured? Did you have some kind of test/ quiz? What was that test/quiz scored out of? The more detail you can give the examiner the better.

TOP TIP: NOT SHOOTING YOURSELF IN THE FOOT

Examiners will see all answers to each personal investigation together. Therefore, you need to make sure that what you say in one answer is the same as in another. If you say that you used a quota sample in one question, then you need to make sure that what you said carries through into your other answers. For example, if you are asked to refine your sample, you need to make improvements to the quota sample you used, not talk about improving opportunity sampling. This sounds obvious but it's a mistake many students make if they didn't conduct their research correctly – or at all! However, because you've already explained something in a previous question, you don't need to explain it again in the next one.

Another possible question in personal investigations is a question that asks you to find a flaw in your research and to refine it. This is applied AO3. When you 'refine' research you could use the following format:

 State an existing **weakness** of the research, e.g. what didn't go well or could have been better?

 Suggest an **adaptation** you could make to improve the research/overcome the weakness, e.g. what could you change to solve the weakness above? Use an example from the research/investigation to ensure it is fully contextualised.

 Explain how your adaptation refines (improves) the research by giving an **advantage** of making this change, e.g. how has what you've done made your research better?

This format can also be used in scenario questions when you are asked to refine a study/piece of research. See page 116 in the second half of this book for real life examples and further tips.

3. Scenario questions

These questions will make up somewhere around one third of the marks on Unit/Component 2. (They also feature in Unit 4 in Wales). For this reason, it is very important that you are as well prepared as you can be for these questions. You will be given a scenario – this is a statement about a fictional 'piece of research' – that will include information to help you respond to the questions associated with it.

TOP TIP: USING THE SCENARIO

You should ensure that you read the scenario carefully. Use a highlighter, or just your pen, to underline key bits of information. All of the information is there for a purpose. It is your job to work out which bits of information will help you with which one of the associated questions.

We suggest doing two things: 1) work out what the variables are (IV and DV) and note them above or below the scenario – this can come in handy later; 2) name the participants – e.g. if they are students, use the word student every time you go to write the word participant in answers to this question.

Far too many students do not read the scenario carefully and then do not gain all the marks on offer. By rushing on to the questions, they have misunderstood the scenario. Any question that uses the phrase 'in this research' or refers to something that occurred in the scenario/study is an AO2 question. Examples of AO2 scenario questions can be seen below.

Give one advantage and one disadvantage of using a correlational study in this research. [2+2]

from WJEC AS Paper, Unit 2, 2018

(i) Identify the experimental design used in this research. [1]

from WJEC AS Paper, Unit 2, 2016

(ii) Explain one disadvantage of using this experimental design in this research. [2]

adpated from WJEC AS Paper, Unit 2, 2016

from Eduqas AS Paper, Component 2, 2017

Briefly explain one strength and one weakness of using a semi-structured interview in this research. [2+2]

from Eduqas AS Paper, Component 2, 2017

Give one strength and one weakness of using the mean score in this research. [2+2]

Although all of these questions could be answered without referring to the scenario, this would be a fatal error! You gain all the marks on offer for including details found in the scenario – by not including them, you limit your marks to the lowest band, as your answer is considered superficial and lacks contextualisation (links to the scenario). The best way to show you what we mean is to give you an example. If we take the questions and scenario below, you could answer them in two ways:

from Eduqas A2 Paper, Component 2, 2018

A Psychology teacher was concerned about the amount of stress her students were experiencing in preparation for their upcoming A level examinations. One month before the examination, she decided to offer her students the opportunity to learn how to meditate. 17 of her students decided to learn how to meditate and practiced meditation for at least 30 minutes per day. 15 of her students decided not to learn how to meditate. As they entered the exam room, she asked each student to rate their stress levels as either 'no stress', 'some stress' or 'very stressed'.

(i) Identify the sampling technique that was used in this research. [1]

(ii) Explain one advantage and one disadvantage of using this sampling technique in this research. [2+2]

Without links to the scenario

(i). Opportunity sample.

(ii). One advantage of using opportunity sampling is that it is quicker and easier than techniques, such as quota or stratified sampling, as there do not have to be a specific number of participants in each group to reflect the target population and the researcher can just use those people who are available at the time. However, one disadvantage is that the sample may contain researcher bias, where the researcher only selects 'helpful' participants that they believe will reflect their aim and expectations within the research.

This response is inadequate as, although it gives an advantage and disadvantage of opportunity sampling, it does not refer to 'this research'. These points would be true of ANY research that uses this type of sample. Therefore, it could only achieve a maximum mark for part (ii) of 1+1. To improve the response, links should be added from the scenario (see an improved example below).

With links to the scenario

(i). Opportunity sample.

(ii). One advantage of using opportunity sampling is that it is quicker and easier than techniques, such as quota or stratified sampling, as there do not have to be a specific number of participants in each group to reflect the target population. In this research the meditation group had 17 students and the control group (who did not meditate) had 15 students. However, one disadvantage is that the sample may contain researcher bias, where the Psychology teacher only selects 'helpful' students for the experimental group, which she believes will have lower levels of stress after meditating.

Real life student examples of scenario questions and examiner comments can be seen on page 116 of this guide.

ACTIVITY

After reading a scenario, you have identified that the participants are '5 year olds' and that the IV is 'whether or not they have been to a zoo' and the DV is the 'number of animals they can name'.

Look at the following paragraph and think about which words or phrases could be substituted to make the answer less generic.

"One confounding variable in this research is that it is possible that some participants have read more books, seen more TV programmes, etc. that could affect their score. It may not be the IV that is affecting the DV, but instead it could be that their score is higher or lower due to life experiences other than the IV."

This response is very generic, but by replacing terms like IV and DV with named information from the scenario, and writing '5 year olds' instead of the word 'participants', it becomes contextualised, allowing access to higher marks.

A contextualised version of the same paragraph (which is not much longer because extra words that do not gain marks – like repeating the question – have been removed) would read:

"It is possible that some 5 year olds have read more books, seen more TV programmes, etc. that could affect the number of animals they can name. It may not be whether or not they have been to the zoo that is affecting the number of animals they can name, but instead it could be that their score is higher or lower due to other unique life experiences."

AO2 in Unit/Component 3: Psychology – Implications in the real world

AO2 only occurs in two ways on Unit/Component 3 and is worth only 25 of the 100 marks available: 5 marks in each behaviour (x3) on Section A – Applications, 10 marks on Section B – Controversies. How to respond to a controversies questions is discussed further on page 97 of this guide.

AO2 in Section A – Applications

The 5 marks allocated to AO2 for each behaviour, can be used in combined AO questions with AO1 or AO3, to make one 15 mark response, or as a separate/discreet 5 mark response. AO2 marks can be allocated to combined questions, for applications, or they can be stand alone:

Briefly explain how social psychological explanations could be applied to modifying bullying behaviours. [5]

from WJEC A2 Paper, Unit 3, 2018

A middle-aged man who recently lost his job has recently started to experience typical symptoms of stress such as increased heart rate, sweaty palms and feelings of anxiety. Outline how one method of modifying behaviour can be applied to any of these symptoms of stress. [5]

from Eduqas A2 Sample Assessment Materials, Component 3

You could be asked to apply any type of explanation (biological, individual differences or social psychological) to any method of modification – but this can never be worth more than 5 marks, unless it is combined with another assessment objective. To this end, it would be sensible for you to think about how you would go about responding to these questions.

The marking scheme suggests that you could gain credit for demonstrating an understanding of the way that the general approach/explanations would be applied to modifying the behaviour. By linking the approach to a broad (or specifically named) method of modification, you will gain further marks. However, you are not required to demonstrate detailed knowledge of specific methods of modifying behaviour, other than the named methods from the specification.

Broadly speaking, you can use the following format for this type of question:

C A brief explanation of the **broad CAUSES of the behaviour** according to the explanation.

A An explanation of **what would need to ALTER or change** to prevent the behaviour according to those assumptions.

T Specific **examples of a THERAPY** that would potentially help to achieve this.

An exemplar response to the first of these three exam questions following this format is as follows:

Briefly describe how biological explanations could be applied to modifying addictive behaviours. [5]

from WJEC A2 Paper, Unit 3, 2018

Exemplar response

Biological explanations of addictive behaviour suggest that all addictions (substance or behavioural) are caused and maintained by biological processes such as neurotransmission and genetics. For example, if the addictive behaviour leads to a release of the pleasure chemical dopamine, in the mesolimbic pathway, the individual is encouraged to repeat the behaviour. Further activation leads to changes in the frontal cortex which affect decision making and memory and contribute to the addiction. Following on from this, biological explanations would suggest that in order to modify the addiction you would need to change the biological processes that are activated when the behaviour is carried out. For example, a drug could be taken that would reduce the amount of pleasure that the individual experiences when they engage in the addictive behaviour and therefore, they would be less likely to repeat it. It could release a small amount of dopamine, so they think they have already had the 'hit' and do not need to engage in the addictive behaviour to get it. For example, agonist substitution could be used to treat addictive behaviour, i.e. heroin addicts could be given methadone as part of a controlled withdrawal.

Guidance on how to address combined AO2/1 or AO2/3 questions can be found on page 86 of this guide.

CHAPTER 3

AO3 Skills: Evaluation

AO3 can be a difficult skill to master, particularly because most students take a thematic approach to their evaluation. For example, you might have learned an acronym or mnemonic of evaluation themes that you use to create ideas for your evaluation answers. Over the years, we have seen many of these examples; Dinosaurs and Tigers Smell Nice (Determinism, Therapies, Scientific nature, and Nature vs. Nurture debate), or SURGED (Scientific, Usefulness, Reliability, Generalisability, Ethics, and Data). Not one of these methods is any better than another and it is not the choice of theme that is important in this skill, but instead, it is all about the style and format of the answer.

What is AO3?

AO3 requires you to analyse, interpret and evaluate a range of scientific information, ideas and evidence. This includes making judgements and reaching conclusions across all papers and developing and refining practical design and procedures in research methods papers.

TOP TIP: FORMAT OF EVALUATION

To gain higher AO3 marks your answer needs to have a logical structure, which includes both depth and range. Depth comes from the use of examples to add detail to your response. Range is achieved by including a number of different themes and ideas in your answer. You should also include a conclusion for questions of 10 marks or more.

What structure should I use in an AO3 answer?

Your answer should include **both strengths/positives and weaknesses/negatives** of the topic at hand. In evaluation you need to carefully balance your time so that you don't have a list like answer that shows lots of ideas which are not elaborated, or an answer that has lots of detail about only two different ideas/themes.

The question below is an example of a past AO3 exam question from Component 1 (Eduqas AS, SAMs).

from Eduqas AS Sample Assessment Materials, Component 1

Evaluate the ethical issues of Watson and Rayner's (1920) research 'Conditioned emotional reactions'. [10]

For this question you would need to include a range of ethical considerations/issues, both in terms of the positives and negatives, which arise from Watson and Rayner's research. Each evaluation response should be tailored to the specific subject material being questioned. For example, Watson and Rayner completed their research prior to the publishing date in 1920. This means that comments about the relevance of today's ethical guidelines are less appropriate within your evaluation. These kinds of comments would be more or less relevant for different pieces of classic research, e.g. guidelines were clearly in place and used for more recent studies such as Loftus and Palmer (1974), and Myers and Diener (1995).

The intention (aim) of the researchers, in classic evidence, could also be a point that could be discussed. For example, Watson and Rayner intended to counter-condition Little Albert, however he was removed from the study by his mother before this could take place. Comments about the fact that this would have made the study more ethical are valid, even though this didn't actually happen. You could also consider the different ethical issues one at a time, applying them to Watson and Rayner with examples. These examples will add depth to your response.

What makes a good evaluation paragraph?

Paragraph structure is key to gaining higher marks in evaluation. Making a statement that is backed up by examples, and then explained in terms of its relative strength/weakness is the way to go. One way you might like to think about writing an evaluation paragraph in any of the exam Units/Components is to use a **sandwich structure**.

 Make your point – state your theme of evaluation and say whether it is a strength or weakness.

 Explain – why is your theme strong/weak in the light of the information you are evaluating? What is good/bad about it?

 Give an example – use some specific information/ knowledge to back up what you are saying.

 Link back to the question – summarise the point/ theme you are evaluating (like a mini conclusion) by stating whether this theme of evaluation is more or less important than the other themes for this research/ approach/explanation/therapy.

How much should I write?

You should **use the number of marks available to determine how much information should be included** in an AO3 question – the same is true of AO1 and AO2.

As a rough rule of thumb, a 10 mark evaluation answer should be at least a side of hand written A4 (or as much as you can write in the time available). Obviously, if you have very big handwriting you will need a longer answer, but if your handwriting is very small it may be slightly shorter. In all of the Units/Components you have roughly 1 minute per mark available in the exam, assuming you need some time to think and to read the questions! Technically, you have 1 minute and 20 seconds, but 20 seconds is not a long time in exam conditions! The examiners know this and will take this into consideration when marking your answers. You should also practice writing as quickly as you can to maximise your time. In constrained exam papers (discussed in AO1) you will be given roughly 20 lines for a 10 mark question – that's 2 lines for each mark, so you need to make them count! Do not ramble or repeat points and try to elaborate and fully explain what you are saying within your answer.

What should I write in my conclusion?

Conclusions in psychology should **draw together the arguments and points you have made** in the rest of the answer. HOWEVER, be careful not to just repeat what you have already said, as this will not gain extra credit. A good conclusion will make a statement about the information that has been evaluated. If there is a quote (applied evaluation: AO2) you should refer to how accurate the quote is, based on the evidence you have provided. Conclusions CAN include new information or make a new/counter point to one previously made in the answer, but they do not have to do this.

Surprisingly, **conclusions do not have to appear at the end of your answer**. You could include mini conclusions (statements about the quality of the information you are evaluating) within your paragraphs. This is useful to know, because if you run out of time in the exam and didn't complete a 'conclusion' at the end of the answer, you will not be penalised for not having ANY conclusions.

Examples of mini conclusions (shown in white) can be seen in Student A's answer below. In this case, they do not have to include a conclusion at the end to access the top mark band. However, Student B has taken a more traditional approach to conclusions but would receive an identical score.

Discuss the ethical considerations of drug therapy or psychosurgery.   *adapted from CPD Materials, 2016*

Student A

One of the major ethical considerations of drug therapy is risks of stress, anxiety, humiliation or pain. Some SSRIs can cause side effects of nausea, headaches and insomnia. These side effects are harmful to the patient. It also reduces effectiveness as the patient may stop taking the drug. A study by Ferguson (2005) found that people treated with SSRIs were twice as likely to commit suicide, suggesting that drug therapy has considerable risks to the patient. The problem with drug therapy is that when the patient stops taking the drugs, their previous symptoms may return, as drugs can be considered to be treating the symptoms of a disorder, such as depression, rather than the cause. This suggests that it is important to recognise the potential harm caused by drug therapies, as they may cause more harm than good, making them unethical.

Another ethical issue is valid consent. People who are prescribed drugs are often in a vulnerable state, due to their psychological health and may not fully understand or be able to acknowledge the risks or side effects associated with the drug. Therefore, the patient is not able to truly give their permission to participate in the therapy. Alternatively, it may be considered that the patient is too ill to make this decision and they could be given drug therapies forcibly within a hospital setting. In this case, valid consent will not have been given, but this may be for the benefit of the patient, who may be a risk to themselves and others. This suggests that, even if valid consent cannot be gained, drug therapies could be considered ethical if they are in the interests of the patient's overall health and wellbeing.

The final ethical issue with drug therapy is possible over-prescription. Some doctors see it as a quick fix, although it may not be appropriate for that particular patient. It should be considered whether the drugs should be used alongside other therapies (such as CBT), or not at all, to suit the individual needs of the patient. If the drug is being used as a short-term solution, it may not be helping the patient in the long term and therefore causing additional problems. This suggests that, overall, the wellbeing of the individual patient may be overlooked by using drug therapies, on the basis of cost and ease of use, which could also be considered an ethical problem.

Student B

One of the major ethical considerations of drug therapy is risks of stress, anxiety, humiliation or pain. Some SSRIs can cause side effects of nausea, headaches and insomnia. These side effects are harmful to the patient. It also reduces effectiveness as the patient may stop taking the drug. A study by Ferguson (2005) found that people treated with SSRIs were twice as likely to commit suicide, suggesting that drugs therapy has considerable risks to the patient. The problem with drug therapy is that when the patient stops taking the drugs, their previous symptoms may return, as drugs can be considered to be treating the symptoms of a disorder, such as depression, rather than the cause.

Another ethical issue is valid consent. People who are prescribed drugs are often in a vulnerable state, due to their psychological health and may not fully understand or be able to acknowledge the risks or side effects associated with the drug. Therefore, the patient is not able to truly give their permission to participate in the therapy. Alternatively, it may be considered that the patient is too ill to make this decision and they could be given drug therapies forcibly within a hospital setting. In this case, valid consent will not have been given, but this may be for the benefit of the patient, who may be a risk to themselves and others.

The final ethical issue with drug therapy is possible over-prescription. Some doctors see it as a quick fix, although it may not be appropriate for that particular patient. It should be considered whether the drugs should be used alongside other therapies (such as CBT), or not at all, to suit the individual needs of the patient. If the drug is being used as a short-term solution, it may not be helping the patient in the long term and therefore causing additional problems.

Overall, it could be argued that drug therapies can do more harm than good and therefore, are unethical. The wellbeing of the individual patient may be overlooked by using drug therapies, on the basis of cost and ease of use. In addition, valid consent is an issue that continues to pose a problem to drug therapies.

AO3 in Unit/Component 1

On Unit/Component 1, evaluation questions can stem around three subtopics – evaluation of therapies, classic research and of the approaches:

Therapies	Classic research	Approaches
Evaluate the therapy including: • Effectiveness • Ethical considerations	Make judgements on a classic piece of evidence including: • Evaluation of methodology, procedures, findings and conclusions • Ethical issues • Social implications	Evaluate the approach including: • Strengths and weaknesses of the approach • Comparison to the other four approaches

Evaluation also features in the debates questions in Component 1 (Eduqas) and Unit 2 (WJEC). However, these are combined Assessment objective questions which we will look at on page 86.

TOP TIP: HOW MUCH SHOULD I LEARN?

In an ideal world you don't want to be 'learning' evaluation in advance of the exam. Evaluation is a skill which you should aim to develop as you progress through the course. If you want to evaluate, for example, therapies with psychological research you will obviously need to learn this, but you should be able to evaluate things like ethics without learning extra material. The key is to ensure that you understand key evaluative terminology, e.g. reliability, validity, data, specific ethical issues and key themes such as nature vs nurture, determinism and scientific nature. Once you know what these mean and you understand the 'thing' you are evaluating, you should be able to create evaluation on the spot.

Evaluating a therapy

Examples of questions within this subtopic can be seen below. Mark allocations vary in different exam years, so it is not possible to 'know' how many marks this type of question will be worth. However, past questions have ranged between 10 and 12 marks. Remember, if the question is worth 10 marks or more, you will need a conclusion. If the question merely asks you to 'evaluate the therapy...' you should include both effectiveness and ethical implications. For higher mark allocations, to give you extra range, you could compare the therapy in question with other therapies to create additional strengths and weaknesses or to form a conclusion to your answer that provides new information.

from WJEC AS Paper, Unit 1, 2018 — *Evaluate drug therapy OR psychosurgery in terms of effectiveness and ethical considerations.* [12]

from WJEC AS Paper, Unit 1, 2016 — *Evaluate cognitive behavioural therapy (CBT) OR rational emotive behaviour therapy (REBT).* [10]

from Eduqas AS Paper, Component 1, 2016 — *Evaluate aversion therapy OR systematic desensitisation.* [10]

If you are including ethical considerations and effectiveness, you could aim to include a positive and a negative point for each theme (where possible – this will be easier for some therapies than others). Do not forget that you need both strengths AND weaknesses for an evaluation question, so even if the therapy seems to have lots of weaknesses (like aversion therapy), you need to make sure that you say something good about it, even if you just say that it is not as unethical or ineffective as another therapy.

Take it further

One way you could expand your response for this type of question (if there is a higher mark allocation – do not do this if it is a low mark question) is to add depth to your response with the 'croque monsieur' method – a croque monsieur is a fancy French toastie where you take a sandwich and add cheese on the top! If you imagine that your evaluation paragraph is the sandwich, you can make it extra fancy/special by making a counterpoint at the end of the paragraph (the cheese to top off your toastie).

For example, you might write a full paragraph about the relative ethical merits of CBT or MBCT, as no physical harm is experienced, and people give consent to take part. You could then finish the paragraph off with a counterstatement, e.g. 'However, although CBT appears to be relatively ethical, clients might face elevated levels of stress and anxiety during their initial sessions when they describe their irrational thoughts and beliefs, which is a minor weakness of the therapy.'

Evaluate the classical research

In this area of evaluation, you can be asked to evaluate the methodology, procedures, findings and/or conclusions of the research.

One method is to tackle evaluation thematically. Methodology and procedures are best evaluated through the terms: reliability, validity and sampling. Comments about internal or external reliability and validity of the methods used and the procedure undertaken, and about population validity, based on characteristics of the sample and sampling technique, are all perfect starting points. Findings and conclusions can be assessed based on their data (qualitative or quantitative and its relative merits/weaknesses), through alternative evidence (no more than two alternative studies are necessary, and NONE are actually a requirement) and social implications. Ethical considerations can be used to evaluate any aspect of the research, either for the participants involved or on the basis of how the research could be used/misused in society.

For each theme you could make a number of points within one giant sandwich (you might only have three sandwiches and a conclusion in this case), or you could break the theme down to make two or three mini sandwiches which are the same 'flavour' (allowing for five/ six bite sized sandwiches). For example, you could have an extended paragraph on validity that encompasses comments about the merits or disadvantages of the method used, the likelihood of validity issues such as researcher bias, demand characteristics or social desirability bias, and the ability to apply findings to different locations/settings. Alternatively, you could make these points into shorter separate paragraphs – however, try not to allow your answer to be list like if you want to be able to access the higher bands.

from WJEC AS Paper, Unit 1, 2017

Discuss the ethical issues and social implications of Loftus and Palmer's (1974) research 'Reconstruction of automobile destruction: an example of the interaction between language and memory'. [8]

from WJEC AS Paper, Unit 1, 2016

Critically evaluate Bowlby's (1944) research 'Forty-four juvenile thieves: Their characters and home-life'. [12]

Looking at the second of these two examples of past questions, you have a broad scope of evaluation that you could address. This question was worth 12 marks, so would require a conclusion (unlike the first of these two past questions – 8 marks, no conclusion needed).

Themes appropriate for discussion when critically evaluating Bowlby include ANY of those discussed above. Evaluation of validity would be appropriate (perhaps less so for reliability, considering the case study methodology), as would discussion of the advantages and disadvantages of Bowlby's sample. Consideration of how data was collected and analysed, in addition to ethical considerations would also have been possibilities. Consideration of social implications, perhaps in the conclusion, would mean that pretty much all bases have been covered. An example of an AO3 question for classic research, with student answers can be seen on page 131 of this guide.

An example of applied evaluation (AO2) that relates to the classic research is as follows:

"Although there are ethical issues and methodological problems, the study of the conditioning of Little Albert is still an influential piece of research."
With reference to the above statement, critically evaluate Watson and Rayner's (1920) research 'Conditioned emotional reactions'. **[10]**

from WJEC AS Paper, Unit 1, 2018

For this question you would use the quote to format your evaluation response including themes that evaluate 'methodological problems' (like reliability, validity and sample issues), in addition to discussing 'ethical issues' and the social implications of the research. Social implications are relevant here because they refer to the 'influence a piece of research' has in society or on other pieces of psychological research. Creating three larger sandwiches, each themed as discussed, with a conclusion that supports/refutes the quote would create a clear structure to the response. Further discussion of how to specifically address applied AO2 questions can be seen on page 34.

Evaluating the approach

These questions can require short or longer answers. They can be based on 'classic' evaluation, where you give strengths and/or weaknesses, or they can require you to 'compare and contrast' an approach to one or more others.

Regardless of the style of question there are a number of themes that you could utilise to create evaluation points, or to compare the approaches. One acronym that might help is DRAINS:

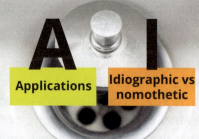

DRAINS

| Determinism | Reductionism | Applications | Idiographic vs nomothetic | Nature vs Nurture | Science |

Taking this approach, where you select relevant themes to expand upon to create evaluation paragraphs, means that you do not have to 'learn' additional material – assuming you understand the approach and its associated therapy (applications). Taking each of these themes, one at a time, you should be able to create strengths and weaknesses within a sandwich structure. It is a good idea to know how each theme can be used either as a strength or a weakness and as such, have the information you need to create the 'bread' of the sandwich. For example, when using determinism as a weakness, a problem with an approach being deterministic is that it does not account for free will and therefore the approach is pessimistic, as it suggests that the individual has no control over their own lives.

from WJEC AS Paper, Unit 1, 2018

Analyse the strengths and weaknesses of the psychodynamic approach. [10]

With this question, determinism is considered a weakness, so the 'bread' could read as follows:

 One weakness of the psychodynamic approach is that it is deterministic.

 This suggests that the psychodynamic approach ignores a person's free will and therefore is considered a pessimistic approach.

What is important to master is the 'filling' within the sandwich. The filling should not be 'floaty' – like a cloud. By floaty we mean that you should not be able to pick up your paragraph and place it into another evaluation essay about an alternative approach. The filling should be 'sticky'. It should be only relevant to that specific approach. You achieve this through ensuring that your filling has examples directly from the topic that you are evaluating. This is particularly important if you are using an acronym to evaluate your approaches, because a number of the approaches share the same strengths or weaknesses. For example, all approaches, with the exception of positive psychology, are deterministic. Therefore, just saying that the approach is deterministic is not enough to gain credit in the higher mark bands. You will need to make sure that you tailor your answer by having 'psychodynamic' flavoured filling in line with the question stem.

A completed sandwich for the above exam question could look like this:

One weakness of the psychodynamic approach is that it is deterministic. This is the case because it assumes that behaviour is affected by unconscious drives, like the tripartite personality, which the individual is unaware of and cannot control. Furthermore, a person's childhood experiences influence personality development, e.g. the way that a child is potty trained can influence a person's temperament and the development of psychological disorders such as OCD. This suggests that the psychodynamic approach ignores a person's free will and therefore is considered a pessimistic approach, a key weakness, as an individual cannot overcome psychological disorders without the help of a trained therapist.

(Extra cheese – see 'take it further' on page 67.) However, one might argue that determinism can also be a strength of the psychodynamic approach because, by reducing the causes of behaviour down to unconscious drives, applications such as dream analysis can be utilised in order to treat depression and OCD.

Common Pitfalls

Some themes within the most commonly used acronyms can appear to be quite similar. For example, students often confuse reductionism and determinism. The key is to be accurate. If you don't know the difference between two themes, only use one of them, or combine them into one paragraph with interchangeable examples, e.g. One strength/weakness is that the approach is both reductionist and deterministic... This suggests that the assumptions made are both oversimplified and pessimistic, key weaknesses of the approach.

As you can see, the sandwich is 'sticky'. It could not be applied to any other approach and is clearly evaluating Freud's ideas. Moreover, by creating a counterpoint at the end of the paragraph (extra cheese) it creates a link into a new theme, creating a clear flow of information that is logical.

TOP TIP: HOW MUCH SHOULD I WRITE?

Realistically, you will not be able to write full paragraphs for all six themes (DRAINS) in an answer that is worth 10–12 marks. Therefore, it would be prudent to include ½ of the themes as counterpoints that are not discussed in detail. Alternatively, you could combine similar points. For example, to elaborate reductionism for the biological or behaviourist perspectives, you could use examples from the nature vs nurture debate. Reductionism concerns an approach ignoring key arguments or oversimplifying ideas. It would therefore be logical to discuss nature and nurture, as examples for these two approaches. However, if you do this, DO NOT repeat the theme again in its own separate paragraph! Think about how you can be accurate and concise, whilst still providing depth and range to your ideas.

Compare and Contrast

For compare and contrast questions you should **include BOTH similarities and differences**. We tend to compare the approaches based on the same themes that we use for classic evaluation of the approaches (DRAINS or similar). You should clearly identify whether your point is a similarity or a difference and use mini conclusions throughout to gain the highest marks. In your mini conclusions we would suggest that you comment on whether the similarity/difference is a strength or a weakness of the approaches you are discussing. This will ensure that you maintain an evaluative style to your answer, instead of just listing points that are the same or different. Examples of these types of questions on past Units/Components include:

from WJEC AS Paper, Unit 1, 2018

Discuss one similarity and one difference between the biological and positive approach.

[4+4]

Compare and contrast the cognitive and psychodynamic approaches in terms of their similarities and differences. [10]

from WJEC AS Paper, Unit 1, 2017

Compare and contrast the biological approach and the cognitive approach. [10]

from Eduqas A2 Paper, Component 1, 2018

Similarities could use the following structure:

S In terms of (insert theme) the (insert name of approach 1) approach and (insert name of approach 2) approach are <u>similar</u>. This is because they both ...

E1 Example from approach 1 ...

E2 Example from approach 2 ...

C Mini conclusion about which approach is better based on this theme (link) and why this is considered a strength or a weakness.

Differences could use the following structure:

D In terms of (insert theme) the (insert name of approach 1) approach and (insert name of approach 2) approach are <u>different</u>.

E1 This is because approach 1 uses/believes/suggests that ...

E2 In contrast, approach 2 would disagree, instead using/believing/suggesting ...

C Mini conclusion about which approach is better based on this theme (link).

If the question is applied evaluation (includes a quote – see examples below) you should also link to that quote at the end of each point (link). You will still respond to these questions in exactly the same way as you would a standard compare and contrast response. Examples of applied AO3 are:

from WJEC AS Paper, Unit 1, 2016

'The biological approach may be more scientific than the psychodynamic approach. However, the psychodynamic approach still has some advantages over the biological approach.'
With reference to the above statement, compare and contrast the biological and psychodynamic approaches in terms of their similarities and differences. [10]

from Eduqas AS Paper, Component 1, 2017

A teacher was asked which approach was the best one: biological or psychodynamic. Using your knowledge, prepare the teacher's answer by comparing and contrasting the biological and psychodynamic approaches. [10]

Planning your answer to these questions is important. Even if you just do a quick table of similarities and differences before you start, it will help you to order and structure the information you have. For example, if you take the final question above and the DRAINS themes, you could do a quick table:

PLAN	Determinism	Reductionism	Applications	Ideographic / Nomothetic	Nature / Nurture	Scientific nature
Biological	Similar	BOTH	BOTH	Different	BOTH	Different
Psychody-namic						

Having completed this table, you can then begin to structure your response. You need AT LEAST one similarity and one difference to meet the criteria for the question. Therefore, it would be sensible to make the first paragraph a similarity and the second a difference, and then go from there. Looking at the table above you can see that there is only one theme that is clearly similar – they are both deterministic. Although, you could argue that reductionism, application and the nature side of the debate are also broadly similar, in that they both ignore some influences on behaviour (psychodynamic less so), they both have therapies that can improve lives (although psychodynamic are used much less frequently and are considered less effective) and they both accept that nature plays a role (at some level) in behaviour. Bearing this in mind, for 10 marks, you could start with determinism and then move on to scientific nature. To save time, you could also combine ideographic/nomothetic into the science point.

Exemplar difference

In terms of scientific nature, the biological approach and psychodynamic approach are different. This is because the biological approach uses methodologies such as lab experiments and brain scans to understand human behaviour. For example, Raine et al. used MRI scans to investigate the brain abnormalities of murderers. In contrast, the psychodynamic approach would disagree with this methodology, instead taking an ideographic approach by utilising methods such as clinical interviews and case studies. For example, Bowlby was able to investigate 44 juvenile thieves using a case study at the London Guidance Clinic. Therefore, when the teacher is asked 'which is best', he/she might respond by suggesting that the biological approach has the advantage over the psychodynamic approach as it better meets the aims of Psychology as a science.

As you write each paragraph you can the cross out the themes as you have written them or included them within other paragraphs. This will prevent you from repeating yourself and help to create a clear flow of information. When a theme is both similar and different, you should try to create balance within your response with what we call a 'double point'. Start with how they are similar and then create a counterpoint within the same paragraph. An example of this can be seen on the next page.

Exemplar 'double point'

In terms of applications the biological approach and psychodynamic approach are both similar and different. They are similar because they both have therapies that can help to improve peoples' lives. The biological approach utilises drug therapies to resolve imbalances in neurotransmitters, whereas the psychodynamic approach uses therapies such as dream analysis as part of a wider psychoanalysis. However, the difference between these two approaches is that the applications of the biological approach are much more widely respected and utilised by the medical community. For biological therapies such as anti-depressants the NHS reports a success rate of between 40–60%. However, psychoanalysis is considered a less useful therapy (a key difference) because even examples of Freud's own cases, e.g. Anna O and Wolfman, were unable to overcome their 'hysteria' and depression. Therefore, the teacher could conclude that the biological approach 'was the best' because it meets the aims of psychology, to improve the lives of humans, better than the psychodynamic approach.

Because this style of paragraph includes mini conclusions at the end of each point, you do not need a separate paragraph to conclude your response if you are running out of time. However, if you wish, you could make a short statement at the end of an applied compare and contrast response that refers back to the quote, in this case, which summarises which approach 'is best'.

AO3 in Research Methods papers

There are very few pure AO3 marks available in research methods papers – most evaluation will be applied (AO2) where it is linked to a scenario, your own personal investigations or Milgram/Kohlberg (see previous section for details on how to respond to AO2 questions). Here are some questions from past exam papers:

from Eduqas A2 Paper, Component 2, 2018

Explain two weaknesses of conducting research on-line.   *[3+3]*

Discuss the strengths and weaknesses of using brain scans in psychology. [6]

from Eduqas A2 Paper, Component 2, 2018

Explain one strength of conducting research on-line. [3]

from Eduqas AS Paper, Component 2, 2017

Justify why cross-sectional studies might be more appropriate than longitudinal studies when conducting research in psychology. [6]

from Eduqas A2 Paper, Component 2, 2017

Explain one advantage and one disadvantage of opportunity sampling. [4]

from WJEC AS Paper, Unit 2, 2016

Briefly explain one disadvantage of an independent groups design. [2]

from WJEC AS Paper, Unit 2, 2017

Evaluate research which is conducted in the field. [6]

from WJEC AS Paper, Unit 2, 2017

Bearing in mind that these papers are constrained, where you have two lines for each mark available, you need to ensure that your evaluation is accurate and concise. Going on and on about something is unlikely to achieve a high score. Themes that are most simply applied to evaluation of research methods are reliability and validity. As a general rule, when something has high validity, the reliability is low and vice versa (it's not entirely this simple, but it gives you a good starting point). It may be useful to consider reliability and validity being at the two ends of a see-saw.

Validity   Reliability

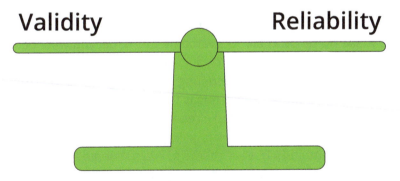

Generally speaking, at the validity end you have more natural locations for research that use face-to-face methodologies, like interviews. These settings illicit more realistic behaviour but are harder to replicate (so they lack reliability). At the other end of the scale, laboratory settings, standardised procedures and methods (like experiments) that require participants to complete identical tasks tend to have high reliability, but at the same time they are unlikely to be reflective of real life (they lack validity). Using reliability and validity (or validity issues, like researcher and social desirability biases) can become the basis of most strengths and weaknesses of locations, methodologies and/or sampling techniques. An exception to this is correlation, where you will need to learn the specific strengths and weaknesses of this methodology as it does not follow the normal pattern.

AO3 on Unit/Component 3: Implications in the real world

There is only one type of pure evaluation question on this Unit/ Component: evaluate the explanation(s) or method of modification. The question (assuming it is not a combined AO – see page 86) is worth 10 marks. You will need to evaluate one or more explanations/ methods of modification. Because this question is worth 10 marks, you WILL need a conclusion – the only exception to this is when the marks are allocated as 5+5.

Evaluating the explanation(s) of behaviour

For these questions you will need to make it clear to the examiner exactly which explanation you are actually evaluating, but you should not describe it. This is because you could have learned a whole range of different explanations that fit under the subheadings of biological, individual differences or social psychological explanations. Remember that in an AO3 question, you get 0 marks for a description of the explanation, but without some reference to its assumptions/beliefs it would make no sense at all. To overcome this issue, you will need to embed very brief descriptions into your evaluation paragraphs to show HOW the evidence you are presenting is a strength or a weakness. One way that you can go about this is to use the sandwich structure – but adapt it so that your example relates back to the explanation.

 Point – STATE your theme of evaluation and say whether it is a strength or a weakness.

 Evidence – provide some kind of statement or EVIDENCE (like a supporting/refuting study/ explanation) to back up the point you have made.

Explain – use some specific information/knowledge about the explanation to back up what you are saying – HOW does the point above support or refute some of the core assumptions/beliefs of the explanation?

Link back to the question – summarise the point/theme you are evaluating (like a mini conclusion) perhaps linking to the next point – WHY is this a strength/weakness?

To evaluate the explanations, you will need supporting/refuting studies for each explanation. You can use the alternative explanations as refuting evidence (being as you already have to learn them) and utilise the skill of evaluating the quality of the evidence presented (e.g. by discussing reliability or validity issues). The idea of how to evaluate the quality of the research you present can be seen in the exemplar paragraphs below.

Evaluate two individual differences explanations of addictive behaviour. [10]

from Eduqas A2 Paper, Component 3, 2018

Exemplar paragraphs

One strength of Eysenck's resource model of addiction is that it has supporting evidence. Gossop and Eysenck (1980) researched over 200 drug addicts and found that addicts had high psychoticism (P) and neuroticism (N) scores, but lower extroversion and impulse control than the control group. This supports Eysenck's original assertion that an addiction develops because it fulfils a need relating to the individual's personality profile, as they are more likely to participate in maladaptive behaviours without considering the consequences (P) and as part of a self-medication against high levels of stress and anxiety (N). Therefore, it can be suggested that Eysenck's model has wider academic credibility.

Additionally, supporting evidence from Dalley et al. (2007), who found that impulsive rats (P) increased their cocaine intake more than low impulsivity rats, adds scientific rigour to Eysenck's theory. The problem with personality research conducted on humans who are addicts is that they are known to be prone to lying (as it is one of the characteristics of addictive behaviour). As a result, it is difficult to be sure of the validity of Gossop and Eysenck's self-report study. However, the fact that Dalley et al. used rats, who are not prone to demand characteristics, strengthens Eysenck's claims. The fact that addicted rats show similar characteristics to human participants allows us to accept that Eysenck's resource model of addiction is accurate/reliable.

TOP TIP: CONCLUDING 'BEHAVIOURS' EVALUATION QUESTIONS

When you conclude a behaviours evaluation question, one thing you could consider is introducing a new point around the topic of a diathesis-stress approach or using the nature vs nurture debate. It is fair to say that almost all behaviours could be attributed to a combination of both biological and social influences. The idea here is that you are born with a genetic/biological predisposition to the behaviour that is then 'triggered' by environmental stimuli, such as a stressful life event. Moreover, psychological disorders like schizophrenia often have a comorbidity element – where a person suffers from more than one disorder at the same time, and cause and effect are difficult to establish. Because this is the case, you could suggest that taking a more holistic approach to explaining behaviour may be more appropriate for almost all behaviours.

As you can see, the two full paragraphs above have only used two studies and knowledge of the explanation is embedded into the first paragraph in the second 'filling' of the sandwich. In the case of this question, you should then move on to evaluating a second individual differences explanation of addiction, before concluding which is most appropriate or commenting on comorbidity as part of a new summarising point (see top tip and exemplar below).

Exemplar conclusion

Overall, it can be concluded that addiction is a complex picture. By only considering individual difference explanations, the issue of comorbidity is ignored. Conway et al. (2006) found that patients with mood or anxiety disorders are twice as likely to suffer from a drug disorder, and vice versa. Potential reasons are 3-fold: 1) Drug abuse causes addicts to experience one or more symptoms of another mental illness (marijuana is linked to schizophrenia); 2) Mental illnesses can lead to drug abuse (individuals abuse drugs as a form of self-medication); and 3) Both drug addiction and other mental illnesses have overlapping factors such as underlying brain deficits, genetic vulnerabilities, and/or early exposure to stress or trauma. As a result of this, it can be concluded that individual differences explanations of addiction, when considered alone, are reductionist. They are an oversimplification that ignores the role of genetics and social psychological factors, and as such, they only paint a partial picture of the causes of addictive behaviour.

As you can see in the exemplar above, this type of conclusion could be used/adapted to any explanation of addiction and as such is a good 'go to' point for an extended conclusion. Using something like this, in addition to two clear paragraphs to evaluate each explanation (for this particular question), will give you the depth and range of information required of the top band.

NOTE: *Please note that these are examplers and only a suggested approach. You would have approximately 15 minutes to answer this question under exam conditions.*

Evaluating methods of modification

Examples of past questions can be seen below:

from Eduqas A2 Paper, Component 3, 2017
Evaluate one method of modifying autistic spectrum behaviours.   [10]

from Eduqas A2 Paper, Component 3, 2017
Evaluate one method of modifying bullying behaviours.   [10]

from WJEC A2 Paper, Unit 3, 2017
Discuss the strengths and weaknesses of one method of modifying addictive behaviours.   [10]

One important thing to note is that (although you can't see this in the above examples) the method of modification can be named directly. This means that you need to know 10 marks of evaluation for BOTH methods of modification. Because you can be specifically asked about, for example, anger management OR restorative justice as methods of modification for criminal behaviours, you need to know BOTH equally well.

Examples of themes for evaluation of the methods of modification include:

- Effectiveness (academic support) – two/three specific examples.

- Ethical implications – risks to people who undergo the method of modification.

- Social and economic implications – potential to improve society by removing the behaviour or costs of the method, either financial or in terms of implications for society if they are ineffective.

If you were to follow this as a rough guide, you would have four/five paragraphs, plus you would need a conclusion. This should be ample for 10 marks – assuming that what you have written is correct and makes sense! One thing you could do in your conclusion is compare the relative success of the therapy with an alternative. For example, you could use a piece of academic support from the other method to show whether the method you are evaluating is more or less effective for that behaviour. Alternatively, you can even use your knowledge from different units – just because Unit/Component 1 is over and seems but a distant memory, this doesn't mean that your knowledge of the therapies, like psychosurgery for addiction or schizophrenia, wouldn't be relevant.

CHAPTER 4

Combined AO Questions

What is a combined AO question?

A combined AO question is an exam question that has allocated some marks to one skill and other marks to a different skill. You won't be able to tell how many marks there are for each skill from the question, but there are rules which mean that the number of marks is always the same, for some question types.

TOP TIP: CONCLUDING 'BEHAVIOURS' EVALUATION QUESTIONS

To gain high marks you need to balance the type of information you put into your exam answer to fit the skills being assessed. A quick guide to the skills of some of the combined AO questions are as follows:

Contemporary debates:	AS Level 20 marks	10 AO1 and 10 AO3
	A Level (in England ONLY) 24 marks	12 AO1 and 12 AO3
Controversies:	25 marks	10 AO2 and 15 AO3

AO1 and AO3: Contemporary Debates

At AS, AO1 is worth 10 marks and AO3 is worth 10 marks, to create a 20 mark essay. At A level, (England only) AO1 is worth 12 and AO3 is worth 12, making a 24 mark essay. In essence, the skills you require for these essays remain the same, only the amount of depth, detail and accuracy required differs between AS and A level. Remember, 4 marks is only an extra 5 minutes, so there really isn't that much difference between the two.

AO1 in the debate

AO1 (knowledge) marks are allocated to the examples of psychological theory and research that you include within your debate. Any inclusion of psychological studies to back up your points and any factual information that is pertinent to the debate is marked as AO1. To gain all the marks on offer, you are aiming to carefully select and use exemplars to support the points you make. You should also aim to be accurate and thorough, whilst including both depth and range. Use of relevant terminology will also be rewarded.

AO3 in the debate

AO3 (evaluation) marks are allocated to your discussion and debating skills. Links to the question stem (including any statement or quote) are all marked as AO3. In addition, comments about social, economic and ethical implications of the debate are credited under this AO. Furthermore, your conclusion(s) make up a significant part of your AO3 score.

Formatting the debate

You should aim to frame your response with AO3. Imagine you are creating a picture: the ideas that create the debate are the frame (AO3) and the picture/content in the middle is AO1. You are aiming to create a comic strip that includes lots of framed pictures that follow a logical sequence of events.

The sequence is determined by the question, particularly if there is a quote. In your mind you should have lots of 'pictures' or ideas about what could be included in a particular debate, but you will order that information in a way that suits the question.

For example, in the cognitive debate, the reliability of EWT (Eye Witness Testimony), you might have pictures such as 'leading questions', 'flashbulb memories', 'face recognition', 'the role of emotion' and 'the cognitive interview'. You wouldn't want to place these pictures into your comic in a random order as it would make no sense. You should order the information logically, depending on the questions stem.

 Common Pitfalls

DO NOT be tempted to learn essays for the debates that you will just regurgitate in the exam. Although this could sometimes work (for example, if there is no quote) it most often leads to lower marks. You must create a 'story' for the examiner that follows a logical flow of information and comes to some sort of conclusion about the debate as a whole.

from Eduqas AS Paper, Component 1, 2016

'Eye-witness misidentification is the greatest contributing factor to wrongful convictions proven by DNA.' The Innocence Project. With reference to psychological knowledge, discuss whether we should rely on the testimony of eye-witnesses. [20]

In this case, the question stem implies that EWT is unreliable. Therefore your 'comic strip' should start with pictures/information (AO1) that supports this statement, e.g. 'leading questions' or negative consequences of 'emotion' such as repression. It should then swing back and forth between the different sides of the argument to create a story that is concluded in relation to the quote. Each picture should be 'framed' with AO3 as a narrative. Below is an example of an opening paragraph in response to the above question that is colour coded to show how AO1 can be framed with AO3.

Exemplar paragraph

AO1 = White

AO3 = Grey

Eye-witness misidentification could occur as a result of leading questions and post-event information. Loftus and Palmer concluded that memory is made up of two components: information gleaned during the event itself and post-event information. Post-event information is any information that is given after the event occurred, such as the use of more (smashed) or less severe (contacted) verbs in questions about estimation of speed in a collision. They suggested that a person only has one memory and so a person may mistakenly misidentify suspects, on the basis of information given to them as part of the interview process. This would suggest that we should NOT 'rely on the testimony of eye-witnesses'. A real-life case that supports this claim is the case of Ronald Cotton. He was misidentified as a rapist when his 'victim' was given post-event information through an e-fit process and unconscious reinforcements from officers who believed Ronald to be the perpetrator. Subsequently, Ronald was released 11 years after sentencing, with the help of the Innocence Project, as it was proved with DNA, that he was wrongfully convicted.

In order to 'join' different pictures of the story together, you can use more traditional evaluation or comment on the social, economic or ethical implications of the previous picture. For example, after writing the paragraph above, you could then evaluate Loftus and Palmer's work or make comments about how another picture (like the cognitive interview) would overcome the issues you have identified (by resolving the problems with police questioning). This link helps you to create the back and forth motion that you would need within the debate, before introducing the next picture in your comic. It also creates more depth to your evaluation (AO3).

In addition to considering the format of your response, you should seriously consider the importance of the debate. What is the point that is being made? Why is the debate a debate? It should be evident within your response that you know this and that you have carefully considered the implications that the outcome of the debate may have within psychology and society at large – this will again boost your AO3 marks, which are generally harder to attain.

ACTIVITY

Draw out five spider diagrams, one for each debate. On the diagram have a number of arrows/legs:

- Why do psychologists argue about this topic?

- What are the positive implications of the debate (how can it be used to improve lives)?

- What are the negative implications of the debate (how might the research be used to create prejudice or injustice)?

- What is the standard of the methodologies or approaches used as evidence for the debate?

By answering these questions, you will start to gain a deeper appreciation of the debate and begin to improve the quality of your AO3.

The only thing remaining within the contemporary debate is your conclusion. As previously discussed on page 62 conclusions can be interwoven into the response, or, can come at the end in a more traditional approach. One thing to note about conclusions within the contemporary debate is that you should sum up which one of your two arguments is the strongest, e.g. should we or should we not rely on the testimony of eye-witnesses. This conclusion should be based on the weight of the arguments you have presented. There is no real right or wrong answer, but be cautious not to just repeat yourself. One way you can avoid this is to briefly include a new final argument for the side of the debate you feel is stronger and refer back to the quote, e.g. 'in the face of the evidence above, the testimony of eye-witnesses should/should not be relied upon... Moreover, if you also consider xxx, which suggests... then you can conclusively suggest that an eye-witness's testimony is/is not 'the greatest contributing factor to wrongful convictions'.'

NOTE: *Examples of two student responses can be seen on page 142 of this guide.*

AO1 and AO3: Unit/Component 3 – Section A: Applications

These questions would require you to describe and evaluate (or any terminology that has the same meaning as this – see page vii) one or two explanations, or methods of modification. For example, questions could be worded as the following:

Outline and evaluate two biological explanations of ... [20]

> *(i) Describe and assess one method of modification for ...* [10]

> *(ii) Describe and analyse one individual differences explanation of ...* [10]

If you were to be asked a question in this format, you should ensure that you split your time carefully between the two skills. It would be logical to tackle this by describing the explanation or method of modification in question for the marks required. Then you should go on to evaluate the explanation/method of modification in question – like two mini essays that are joined as one response: first describe and then evaluate (do not forget your conclusion). For a question like this that asks for two explanations/methods of modification, to be outlined and evaluated, you should follow the same format, but repeat the process for the second explanation. In this case, your conclusion could perhaps include a comparison between the two explanations/

methods of modification that you have written about. A mini essay plan that follows this format can be seen below:

Outline and evaluate two social psychological explanations of...   *[20]*

- Describe explanation 1 for 5 marks

- Evaluate explanation 1

- Describe explanation 2 for 5 marks

- Evaluate explanation 2

- Conclusion – Compare the two explanations; which is a better explanation and why? Do BOTH explanations lack anything? Are they reductionist?

AO1/3 and AO2: Unit/Component 3 – Section A: Applications

On this Unit/Component, the 5 marks of AO2 (per application/ behaviour) can be combined with either AO1 or AO3 for that section. This is usually achieved through a scenario or a quote, where you will apply either knowledge (AO1) or evaluation (AO3) of explanations or methods of modification.

Examples of past questions that combine AO1 with AO2 for 15 marks (10 + 5) are:

Natalie likes going to the casino. At first, she would go only once a month. Now she goes at least four times a week. She realises she has an addiction to gambling and is seeking help. Her psychologist has suggested a number of different methods of modifying this behaviour. Describe one method of modifying addictive behaviour with reference to Natalie.   *[15]*

from Eduqas A2 Paper, Component 3, 2018

Ronald has not been feeling the same lately. He told his friend Rory what he has been experiencing. Rory suggested that the behaviours Ronald is showing could be characteristics of schizophrenia. Describe the characteristics of schizophrenia that Ronald may have told Rory he was experiencing.   *[15]*

from Eduqas A2 Paper, Component 3, 2018

from Eduqas A2 Paper, Component 3, 2017

Caroline has autism. Her dad wanted to understand more about the condition. A psychologist informed him about social psychological explanations of the behaviour. Describe two social psychological explanations for autistic spectrum behaviours referring to Caroline in your response. [15]

from Eduqas A2 Paper, Component 3, 2017

Louise has been bullied in the workplace. She has been subjected to behaviour which is intended to hurt her emotionally and physically. With reference to Louise, describe one social psychological explanation of bullying behaviours. [15]

from Eduqas A2 Paper, Component 3, 2017

In 2014/15 stress accounted for 43% of all working days lost due to ill health (HSE, 2015). With reference to this statistic, describe one biological and one individual difference explanation of stress. [15]

To address this type of question (AO1/2) you should ensure that the bulk of your answer is a description of the explanation(s) in question, or the method of modification. There should be enough information to gain 10 marks. Advice about what you should include in this content can be seen on page 24. In order to get your five AO2 marks, you will need to apply your descriptions to the quote or scenario. This means writing some information (description – AO1) and then relating it directly to the scenario (application – AO2), then repeating this process. An example of an applied paragraph that begins a response to the following question can be seen below.

from WJEC A2 Paper, Unit 3, 2017

Signs of fruit machine addiction include: the belief that one is not gambling with real money; the development of a personal 'relationship' with the machine; and a feeling of irritation if someone else is playing that machine. Addicts may play for longer than they planned and lie about how much money they have won or lost.

Describe how two explanations of addictive behaviours can be applied to the above scenario. [15]

Exemplar paragraph

AO1 = White

AO2 = Grey

One explanation of addictive behaviour is cognitive biases and maladaptive heuristics. This explanation suggests that faulty internal processing causes fruit machine/gambling addiction. Addicts show attentional biases, by focusing on the positive aspects of their addiction and ignoring the potential negative consequences. For example, a gambler will take credit for a win (dispositional attribution) but attribute failure to situational factors (self-serving bias), like someone else playing on 'their' machine. Faulty processing also occurs due to the development of maladaptive heuristics. This is why addicts play for longer than planned and lie about how much money they have won or lost. Two examples of heuristics that contribute to gambling are: 1) Representativeness – The belief that random events have a predictable pattern, because they focus on a series of events from a small sample (gambler's fallacy). This would explain why fruit machine addicts feel irritation when someone is playing at 'their' machine, as they believe that the machine is easier to win on than any other – they and the machine are friends, the addict trusts the machine. 2) Availability – The idea that something is more likely to happen because they can remember hearing about it (so it is easier to recall/remember). Toneatto (1999) found that typical cognitive distortions of gamblers included selective memory, superstitious beliefs and an illusion of control, which is consistent with the symptoms described in the scenario where the addict believes they are not gambling with real money.

In the example above, you can see that the AO2 (links to the scenario) has been interwoven into the response. They are not just placed on the end or the beginning, but they are part of the answer as a whole. This technique will be better, but if you do forget to apply, adding links to the end of your description is better than not adding any links at all.

Examples of past questions that combine AO3 with AO2 for 15 marks (10 + 5) are:

from WJEC A2 Paper, Unit 3, 2018

Siân is a teaching assistant supporting children with autistic spectrum disorders. She supports two children. David struggles with social interaction and expressing his emotions and Clare struggles with communication skills. With reference to the scenario, evaluate methods of modifying autistic spectrum behaviours that Siân could use to support David and Clare.   [15]

from WJEC Paper A2, Unit 3, 2017

Mrs Davies is the new headteacher in a large secondary school where bullying is a problem. She decides to ask a psychologist for advice on methods of modifying bullying behaviour. With reference to this scenario, evaluate the effectiveness of methods of modifying bullying behaviour.   [15]

from Eduqas A2 Paper, Component 3, 2017

Emily is a support worker for James who has demonstrated criminal behaviour. A psychologist suggested that she might look at social psychology for potential explanations. Evaluate one social psychological explanation of criminal behaviours in order to help Emily understand James's behaviour.   [15]

from WJEC A2 Paper, Unit 3, 2018

Some psychologists would suggest that individual differences explanations do not fully explain schizophrenia. With reference to this statement, evaluate individual differences explanations of schizophrenia.   [15]

from Eduqas A2 Paper, Component 3, 2018

Mehdi is highly stressed about his examinations, driving test and other personal issues. Various methods of modifying this behaviour have been suggested to him. Evaluate one method of modifying Mehdi's stress.   [15]

As you can see from the extensive examples above, this type of combination question has been very popular – where AO2 has been paired with evaluation (AO3). There are two styles that have been used in exam questions so far, scenario questions based on a 'fictional client' and statement questions that create a basis for discussion and debate.

One way that you can go about responding to this type of question is to utilise the sandwich structure discussed on page 78. You will need to make it clear to the examiner exactly which explanation/method of modification you are actually evaluating, but you should not describe it. In addition to using evaluative language and terminology, it is good practice to refer back to the scenario or statement at least once in every paragraph. Sometimes you will be able to do this quite easily, at other times it might be trickier. Furthermore, you should make sure that you balance your answer with strengths AND weaknesses, and if you are evaluating more than one explanation/method, you should ensure that you split your time evenly so that you address the whole question.

Individual differences explanations of schizophrenia are incomplete and lack supporting evidence. With reference to this statement, evaluate two individual differences explanations of schizophrenia. [15]

Exemplar paragraph WITHOUT application (AO2)

One strength of the Psychodynamic explanation for Schizophrenia (the Schizophrenogenic mother) is that it has supporting evidence. Kasanin examined hospital records and found that 33 out of 45 cases of people with schizophrenia also had overprotective mothers. Furthermore, Waring and Ricks concluded that mothers of children with schizophrenia were more often than not withdrawn, incoherent and anxious. Both these studies support the Schizophrenogenic mother explanation, as the 'cold, distant, overprotective' stereotype is met, therefore the explanation has wider academic credibility.

Most students tend to lean towards using supporting or contradictory evidence as evaluation points. The above paragraph uses the sandwich structure and embeds 'knowledge' of that explanation within the evaluation point in the 'bread' of the sandwich. The filling is made up of the supporting research. In a straight evaluation question this paragraph would be adequate, however in a combined AO question this paragraph would not receive any credit for AO2. Therefore, it is your job to add in statements/suggestions to link back to the statement. You don't have to do this all the way through the paragraph, because there are only 5 marks of AO2 available across the whole essay, however you should try to include a link at least once per point you are making.

Common Pitfalls

A common mistake that students make when answering these questions is that they spend time describing the explanation or

from WJEC and Eduqas CPD materials, 2017

method of modification that they are about to evaluate. This information feels necessary for your answer to make sense, but actually gains no marks. To avoid this pitfall you should practice embedding knowledge into your evaluation so that it is creditworthy.

See page 78 for an example of a sandwich which does this.

Exemplar paragraph WITH application (AO2)

AO2 = Grey

One strength of the Psychodynamic explanation for Schizophrenia (the Schizophrenogenic mother) is that it has supporting evidence. This directly contradicts the statement. Kasanin examined hospital records and found that 33 out of 45 cases of people with schizophrenia also had overprotective mothers. Furthermore, Waring and Ricks concluded that mothers of children with schizophrenia were more often than not withdrawn, incoherent and anxious. Both these studies support the Schizophrenogenic mother explanation, as the 'cold, distant, overprotective' stereotype is met, therefore the explanation has wider academic credibility. This suggests that the statement is inaccurate as there does appear to be supporting evidence for individual differences explanations of schizophrenia.

In addition to embedding links to the statement (AO2) across your whole response, you should also refer to it in your conclusion(s). One way that you may want to consider concluding applied evaluation responses is by comparing the explanation/method in question to an alternative. It is important that you do not describe these other explanations but mentioning them, to provide a juxtaposition to your main arguments, showcases your broader psychological knowledge.

Exemplar conclusion WITH application (AO2)

AO2 = Grey

Based on the evidence provided above it can be concluded that the statement is correct. Whilst the explanations do have supporting evidence, partially disputing the quote, they do in fact appear incomplete. This is because they fail to recognise alternative biological explanations for schizophrenia, such as the role of dopamine and/or cannabis use. Moreover, they also fail to recognise social psychological explanations such as the role of dysfunctional families and expressed emotion. This suggests that individual differences explanations, when considered alone, are an oversimplification of the causes of schizophrenia and that a more appropriate approach would be to use a diathesis-stress model.

AO2 and AO3: Unit/Component 3 – Section B: Controversies

There are five different controversies: cultural bias, ethical costs of conducting research, non-human animals, scientific status and sexism. For each controversy you need to understand the issue at hand and know why it is considered controversial – why is there debate in this topic? You will need to be able to apply your broader psychological knowledge and understanding to the controversies (AO2) and make judgements/draw conclusions from a psychological perspective (AO3). In reality, your own opinion about the controversy is irrelevant; you need to use everything you have learned to show what the argument is and then make a statement about it.

You might find that this question is the hardest you will answer in the whole of A level psychology. It is synoptic – so it takes everything you have learned over two years and gets you to apply it to a controversy that psychology faces as a subject. It is, in essence, the true meaning and purpose of psychology, because psychology is not just an approach or a therapy, it is an all-encompassing subject that aims to improve people's lives.

TOP TIP: EXPLORING THE CONTROVERSY

Within each controversy there are four areas of 'exploration'. Questions can be based on the controversy as a whole, or just on one aspect. It is therefore important that your response does not use rote learning (memorisation of information based on repetition) and that you tailor your response accordingly (see 'structuring your answer' on page 100).

To find out what the 'areas of exploration' are you should look at the specification:

- For students in Wales (Page 19)
  http://bit.ly/2OV5qyU

- For students in England (Page 15)
  http://bit.ly/2TvePfn

Examples of two exam questions from the 'ethical costs of conducting research' controversy can be seen below. These examples highlight how the same topic can be assessed in two different ways as they focus on different areas of exploration.

from Eduqas A2 Paper, Component 3, 2017

'Psychological research continues to involve ethical costs to society and individual human participants.' To what extent do you agree with this statement? Justify your answer. [25]

from WJEC A2 Paper, Unit 3, 2017

'Good research means never having to say you are sorry.' (Reason and Rowan, 1981). With reference to psychological research, discuss the advantages and disadvantages of having ethical guidelines. [25]

*Eduqas only

Ethical costs of conducting research:

❖ benefits to society (and the economy*)

❖ individual participants

❖ potentially negative consequences for society

❖ use of ethical guidelines (Wales) / risk management techniques used by Psychologists (Eduqas)

The four areas of exploration for this controversy can be seen in the box above. The first of these two exam questions, combines the second and third areas of exploration – costs to individual participants AND potentially negative consequences for society. The second exam question focuses on the last area of exploration – use of ethical guidelines.

If you were to write a generic response about ethical costs of conducting research, you will score some marks, but you are unlikely to attain the top band because you will not have shown the accuracy required. Adding in irrelevant information, or not adapting your knowledge to suit the question stem, will put you at a big disadvantage. Not only do you have to consider the areas of exploration being addressed, but you also need to balance your answer to ensure that you access marks for both AO2 and AO3: 10/25 marks are allocated as AO2 and 15/25 are allocated as AO3.

AO2 in controversies

AO2 in these questions refers to the application of evidence, so each time you use a core idea/theme/piece of research (what you might think of as knowledge) you will be awarded AO2 marks if you have linked it to the question in hand. Any links to the statement/quote (if there is one) are also AO2. Moreover, AO2 consists of skills which are more difficult to quantify – you won't be able to read an answer and 'see' these components, but they will become apparent throughout the entirety of your answer. Unseen skills, like the depth and range of your examples, in addition to selecting examples that are appropriate and using key terminology are all considered AO2. Therefore, if your essay is logical, has a range of ideas and selects material appropriately you will gain a high AO2 score.

AO3 in controversies

AO3 is your discussion of the controversy. Use of evaluative language, creating a clear argument, developing your points so that the debate is well balanced and carefully concluding the debate is all important if you want to gain a high score. You should ALWAYS include both sides of the debate, even if the question/quote leans towards one side. You need to create balance to your answer and draw conclusions (AO3) based on the evidence you have applied (AO2).

Structuring your answer

In an ideal world you should sandwich your arguments/evidence between evaluations. Think of the bread of your sandwich as AO3 and the filling as AO2. To ensure that you have enough AO3 (as it is worth 15 marks out of the 25 available) you should also evaluate the evidence you have provided or explain how/why two points fall on the opposite sides of the debate. In an ideal world you should also create an argument that is to-and-fro rather than dumping all the knowledge for one side of the controversy down and then scribbling down information about the other side separately. You will still get some marks if you do this, but you are unlikely to access the higher mark bands, because your structure and discussion of the debate would not be considered thorough or logical.

Ideally, you should approach controversies in a similar style to contemporary debates, where you have various pictures (pieces of applied evidence) that you should place into a story/comic, to match the question. For example, for the 'ethical costs of conducting research' controversy, you will have four themes (based on the areas of exploration) and within those, you might have 3/4 pictures (pieces of evidence). It is your job to use that evidence in a way that suits the question.

from Eduqas A2 Paper, Component 3, 2017

'Psychological research continues to involve ethical costs to society and individual human participants.' To what extent do you agree with this statement? Justify your answer. [25]

If we take the question above, and consider the four areas of exploration, we would clearly want to start with a picture/evidence from 'potentially negative consequences of research for society'. You will make these points whilst linking back to the question. You would then create a juxtaposition to this point (perhaps 'framed' as evaluation) by using evidence from the 'benefits to society' area of exploration. You will not include as much detail from this theme, but it is important that you make it clear that different psychologists hold different beliefs (hence why this is a controversy at all).

Next you might want to use evidence from the costs to the 'individual participants' area of exploration. By doing this you have addressed both aspects of the question (society and the individual). At this point you would want to evaluate this 'area'. You can do this with generic evaluation points, or you could create a further juxtaposition by explaining that 'ethical guidelines' can help to overcome costs to individual participants. You must make sure that the bulk of your answer is made up of the core themes in the question, but you can still use the other areas of exploration within your answer, as long as they are framed with evaluation.

To conclude (which you MUST do in a controversies essay), you would then sum up which side of the debate is strongest. You can do this based on the evidence that you have presented – summing up the purpose of the debate – or you can introduce a new piece of evidence to back up whichever side of the debate you think is stronger. Both these methods are appropriate and would be awarded AO3 marks. Where there is a quote, as in this case, you should refer to it and respond directly to the question 'To what extent do you agree with this statement?' By doing so, you should be able to gain all the marks on offer, assuming that your evidence and discussion is accurate, thorough and logical.

CHAPTER 5

Questions and Answers

This section of the book adds detail to the previous section, by giving examples of real student responses to real examination questions. This section is not exhaustive and does not include every type of question that can or has been asked. For example, more straightforward questions, such as those based on descriptions of the assumptions (AO1) have not been included. The purpose of this section is to make you aware of some common pitfalls and to give you advice about how poor answers can be improved. There are also some examples of top band responses, to give you an idea of what you should be aiming for in your exams.

AO1

Unit/Component 1 – AO1: Classic Research

In these questions you are required to describe/outline the methodology, procedures, findings and/or conclusions of a study. **You MUST NOT include** details about a part of the study you have not been asked about in these types of questions. You need to be as accurate as possible for these questions, as any irrelevant information will impact on your accuracy and waste valuable time.

from WJEC AS Paper, Unit 1, 2017

Describe the conclusions made by Loftus and Palmer (1974) in their research 'Reconstruction of automobile destruction: an example of the interaction between language and memory'. [6]

Advice: All 6 marks for this question are allocated as AO1 – knowledge. Therefore, the examiner is looking for a thorough response that is accurate. To achieve accuracy, only relevant information about the 'conclusions' of Loftus and Palmer's research are required. Any information about the numerical results of the study, e.g. speeds of the various verbs are not relevant, as they would be considered 'findings' and are not required in this question.

When this question was asked in the exam, the examiners were looking for a description of any of Loftus and Palmer's conclusions. Answers could include:

- Direct quotes from the discussion section of the original article, e.g. 'The way a question is asked can enormously influence the answer that is given.'

- Comments about the long-term effects of the research on participants' perception, e.g. that the effects lasted a week.

- The ideas proposed by Loftus and Palmer about memory, e.g. it is made up of two kinds of information: perception of the event, and information 'after the fact'. These two sources are integrated to form 'one memory'.

- Discussions of Loftus and Palmer's findings in relation to alternative studies, e.g. links to Carmichael et al. (1932) and Daniel (1972) about the role of verbal labels.

Student Answer A

Loftus and Palmer concluded that certain words used can actually alter someone's memory and make them think that things happened more or less severely than they actually did. They also said that memory could be affected over time and the memory therefore becomes less reliable, as it could lead to information being remembered incorrectly.

Examiner feedback: This student has produced a superficial response to this question. It has limited terminology. **2/6 marks** were awarded for this response.

TIP: This student needed to be more precise with their answer. Explaining HOW the verbs altered memory or explaining how memory is created, according to Loftus and Palmer, would have been beneficial. The fact that they failed to mention that there were two experiments that came to different conclusions, was also a drawback of the response that could easily have been addressed.

Student Answer B

Loftus and Palmer concluded that the words used in a leading question could affect the estimation of speed given and therefore the memory. They also concluded that the verb used in the leading question could also alter memory. They said that police, lawyers, etc. need to be more aware of the wording of their questions when interviewing witnesses. Loftus and Palmer concluded that the critical word used, could affect or even alter memory.

Examiner feedback: This response is very repetitive and again, despite appearing slightly longer, it is still considered superficial. Comments about the 'police, lawyers, etc.' are social implications of the research and are not conclusions drawn in the original article of the study, therefore, they are not creditworthy. In addition, the student essentially says the same thing, that leading questions/verbs/critical words affect memory, three times! It therefore also only achieves **2/6 marks** as a 'superficial' response.

Student Answer C

Loftus and Palmer concluded that there is a key link between how we phrase the question, in this case a verb, i.e. 'smash', and someone's memory of an event.

They came up with two reasons for this, the first being response bias. The severity of the verb used would cause the person to bias a more severe recollection of the event.

The second being that leading questions can dramatically and systematically change a person's memory. If this is true, you would expect witnesses to remember things that weren't there. This is true in experiment two, where the smashed category said yes more to seeing glass at the accident, than the control category.

Examiner feedback: This response gives a 'reasonable' description of a 'range' of conclusions, and so achieves **4/6 marks**. Some key terminology is used when referring to 'response bias', which is pleasing.

TIP: To gain those last two elusive marks the candidate could have added details about how memory is created by two forms of information, according to Loftus and Palmer, or referred their second conclusion back to the work of Daniels (1972), by suggesting that memory shifts towards the representation of the verbal label.

Unit/Component 3 – AO1: Explanations of behaviour

AO1

All straight AO1 questions on this Unit/Component are worth 10 marks.

Describe anger management as a technique for modifying criminal behaviours. [10]

from Eduqas A2 Paper, Component 3, 2017

Advice: Make sure that the whole of your answer is descriptive – no evaluation is necessary. Anger management is a technique for reducing anger, originally based on a model put forward by Ray Novaco. It was his view that anger had biological, cognitive and behavioural aspects/elements to it. Comments about this would be creditworthy in this response, as long as they are contextualised to criminal behaviour. There are many different examples of anger management techniques that you could include; a British example would be CALM (Controlling Anger and Learning to Manage it). Essentially, what most systems have is a focus on teaching relaxation techniques with the aim of reducing the biological changes/response to anger, that violent criminals demonstrate. Cognitive restructuring is used to deal with problematic thought patterns. To deal with the behavioural element, assertiveness training is used. While different techniques of anger management might have varying numbers of stages, the principles remain the same: (1) Cognitive preparation, (2) Skills acquisition and (3) Application practice.

Student Answer A

Anger management has two key aims; firstly, a short-term aim, of reducing the level of aggression in prisons, as this is a real issue within the prison system. And secondly, a long term aim of rehabilitating offenders to stop them reoffending.

Anger in prisoners is at an all-time high. They often have cognitive distortions like hostile attribution bias and minimisation. Hostile attribution bias is always perceiving things in a negative way. Minimisation is where you reduce the effect that your crime has. Anger management aims to try and challenge these distortions and make them less aggressive.

There are 3 main aims of anger management as stated by Novaco. Firstly, to reduce the rates of reoffending within prisons. Secondly, to reduce aggression within the individual and help them deal better with stress/anger management. Lastly, to help keep society safer when the criminals are released.

Anger management also uses stress inoculation training to help them deal better in stressful situations and not turn to violence. This starts with conceptualisation, imagining the situation and working out their triggers and how to deal with them. Secondly, skill acquisition and rehearsal. This is where the necessary skills are learned and applied to imaginary scenarios through role play. Lastly, application and follow through, where skills learnt are applied to real life situations in order to reduce stress.

Examiner feedback: A reasonably detailed response, which showed 'reasonable' accuracy. The candidate logically structures notes and illustrates a range of aspects of the technique. There is some repetition and some points could have benefited from greater depth. **7/10 marks**.

TIP: Try to avoid repeating yourself and only include information relevant to the question. Make sure that you use as much technical terminology as possible and illustrate your points with examples that would directly apply to criminal behaviour, as methods like anger management can also be used in other settings. Details about how it is used specifically with criminals would be helpful, as would details about specific programmes, such as CALM.

Student Answer B

There are three main stages, and they are as follows:

Conceptualisation – this is where the patient opens up to the therapist about problems.
Skills acquisition – the patient and therapist work together to find a way to deal with anger – these are coping mechanisms.
Application – the skills learnt are then applied to real life scenarios.

The patients are taught that if they do relapse they can see this as a learning curve and move on from it.

Examiner feedback: The response is brief. It illustrates a basic level of understanding, just enough to pull it out of superficial, and this, in part, is evident by the correct use of terminology. The response lacks depth but does (briefly) make a number of points. **3/10 marks**.

Student Answer C

Anger management is a technique that is used to modify criminal behaviour. The aim of anger management is to reduce aggression in the individual and to reduce the risk of recommitting the crime and being reconvicted.

Anger management has many components which help to modify criminal behaviour. The criminal will participate in cognitive restructuring, where the criminal will learn to challenge their aggressive thoughts. Another component is behavioural strategies. The criminal will learn ways and strategies in which they can control their aggression and criminal behaviour.

Another component of anger management is stress inoculation training (SIT). SIT has 3 parts, which are: conceptualisation, skill acquisition and application. In the first part (conceptualisation), the criminal will work with the therapist to break down their behaviour (criminal behaviour). Both the criminal and therapist will look at the skills that the criminal already has for coping with their behaviour. In the second part of SIT (skill acquisition), the criminal will work on how to develop the skills they have for dealing with their behaviour and they also work on developing new ones. The criminal and the therapist will then work on applying the behaviour and skills in clinical settings and then in real-life situations. In the third section of SIT (application), the criminal will learn how to apply what they have learnt, when aggression, etc. arises.

Anger management is a form of cognitive behavioural therapy which can be used to modify criminal behaviour.

Examiner feedback: The candidate has a clear idea of the method of modification. The description is thorough and accurate. The candidate makes effective use of appropriate terminology. Aspects of the description could have been illustrated to gain further depth. **8/10 marks**.

Component 1 – AO2: Applying the assumptions to behaviour (England Eduqas ONLY)

In England, at A level only, you can be asked to apply one or more assumptions to a 'variety of behaviours'. This means that you should consider knowing how to apply each assumption to at least two different behaviours. If you have studied AS psychology in the first year, you may wish to use 'relationship formation' as one of your two behaviours, as you will already be familiar with this type of question. For your second 'behaviour' you may wish to choose one specific behaviour for all approaches, or different behaviours for different approaches. This second option could be useful, particularly when it comes to the positive approach. Whilst most approaches lend themselves to describing abnormal behaviours such as phobias, depression, schizophrenia, etc., the positive approach is more suited to pro-social behaviours. As such, considering a behaviour like 'giving money to charity', or behaviours such as volunteering, will be simpler to explain using the positive assumptions of free will, goodness and excellence and the good life.

Apply your knowledge of the assumptions of the behaviourist approach to explain one human behaviour. [10]

from Eduqas A level Paper, Component 1, 2016

Advice: In this question, the examiner is looking for you to apply the assumptions, not just to describe them. You must also apply them to ONE HUMAN behaviour. You would be surprised to learn how many students explained multiple behaviours or looked at the behaviour of dogs/rats! If you are sitting this Component at the end of year two, then it would be sensible for you to choose a behaviour you know more about – like any of the three behaviours you learned/are learning for Component 3 (the only exception to this would be if the approach was positive psychology – where a more prosocial behaviour would be easier to apply). You don't need to include all three assumptions (particularly the idea that humans and animals are the same), but you must include at least two, as it asks you to 'apply knowledge of the assumptions...' – plural.

When this question was asked in the exam, the examiners were looking for candidates to write for about 10 minutes. Signposting the assumptions to the examiner – perhaps by underlining key terminology – could also be useful, but is not essential. Any human behaviour was credit worthy. Good answers were likely to include some of the following ideas and terminology:

- Classical conditioning.

- Operant conditioning.

- Social learning theory, including the role of observation.

- The idea that all behaviours are learned (tabula rasa).

- The idea that human behaviour can be measured scientifically, is determined, etc.

NOTE: *Answers should NOT include descriptions of research with non-human animals, e.g. Pavlov or Skinner, unless these have been directly linked/compared to the human behaviour in question.*

Student Answer A

The assumptions of the behaviourist approach are a blank slate, which shows that there is no internal mental content and our mind is a 'tabula rasa'. Any behaviour is learned through our social and environmental surrounding. Another assumption is that we learn behaviour through classical and operant conditioning. Classical conditioning is involuntary, and we learn through making associations, whereas, operant conditioning is voluntary, and we learn through positive and negative reinforcements and punishment. The last assumption is that animals and humans learn in similar ways and that we are able to test on animals in labs and then apply to humans.

Addictive behaviour can be explained through the behaviourist assumptions. Firstly, we learn our association to addictive behaviour through our environment, we are not born addicted to something, because there is no innate previous mental content. Everything is learned and therefore addictive behaviour is learned, and if they can be learned, they can also be unlearned. Secondly, aversion therapy which treats addictive behaviour is based on classical conditioning and learning a stimulus-response link through association. For example, rapid smoking is a form of aversion therapy that works by making a new stimulus-response link, but one which is negative. It works by, for example, getting the individual to take 56 puffs every 10 seconds, until they finish a certain number of cigarettes or they feel sick. It works by making an association of smoking and feeling sick, in order to stop smoking.

In conclusion, addictive behaviour can be explained by the assumptions of the behaviourist approach.

Examiner feedback: Unfortunately, nothing in the first paragraph is creditworthy, because it is all AO1 description of the assumptions, that have NOT been applied to a human behaviour. In the second paragraph, although there is evidence of some terminology, there is a lack of detail on classical conditioning. The answer does not explain how addiction occurs in relation to classical conditioning, it only outlines (towards the end) how aversion therapy works. This description of aversion therapy could gain some marks, if it were applied to classical conditioning and addiction. However, it is not and so is not creditworthy. Moreover, a conclusion is not required in this AO2 response. This response earned **3/10 marks** as it was considered a basic description of addictive behaviour, where exemplars are not always made relevant.

TIP: To improve this answer, the student could have used a clearer structure to their response. If they had taken one paragraph for each of the 3 key themes (classical conditioning, operant conditioning and social learning theory) and applied them to addiction, they would have scored a much higher mark. Using the SEE structure for each paragraph would help:

S   State the assumption.

E   Explain the main causes of the behaviour according to the principles of the assumption – this will be 2 or 3 sentences.

E   Give specific examples of how the characteristics can arise from the behaviour you are describing, e.g. characteristics displayed by the addicted person.

NOTE: *Some sample answers, where the approaches have been applied to a range of different behaviours, can be seen in the following Eduqas online activity:* http://bit.ly/2kvlf0W

Unit/Component 1 – AO2: Applying the approach to a therapy

This type of question requires you to explain how the assumptions of the approach are applied through the main ideology and components of the therapy. You could approach these questions using the NAAN acronym (see page 37).

from Eduqas AS Paper, Component 1, 2016

Explain why a psychologist following the biological approach would consider drug therapy OR psychosurgery as a suitable therapy. [5]

Advice: All five marks for this question are allocated on the basis that the explanation you give about the approach, such as details about the assumptions, is applied directly to the therapy chosen (see page 38 in the first half of this guide for advice on how to structure your responses to this type of question). No marks are gained for describing the therapy, as that is an AO1 skill. Evaluation of the therapy (AO3) is also not required.

When this question was asked in the exam, the examiners were looking for an explanation of how the following ideas relate to either drug therapy, or psychosurgery:

- The idea that a physical cause for illness/disorder requires a physiological treatment.

- Use of the medical model.

- Links to the assumptions of the approach (neurotransmitters or localisation of brain function).

- Examples of different drug therapies OR psychosurgeries to treat specific disorders.

- The effectiveness of the therapy to justify suitability.

- Comparison to other therapies to explain suitability.

Student Answer A

They may consider psychosurgery a suitable therapy as it can deal with depression, schizophrenia, etc., it provides a long-term solution and, in modern procedures, is safe and effective. An example of this is a bilateral cingulotomy, stereotactic surgery where an MRI is used to pinpoint the exact location so less damage is caused. A lesion is made by placing the tip of an electrode or focusing a radiation beam or gamma knife. Rauch et al. found this to be effective in 56% of OCD patients.

Examiner feedback: Overall, this is a superficial application of the student's knowledge to why biological psychologists might consider psychosurgery to be a suitable therapy. It does not directly answer the question asked. To improve the answer, the student could have linked to the assumptions of the approach and/or compared psychosurgery's effectiveness to other types of treatment to explain its suitability. **1/5 marks** were awarded for this response.

Student Answer B

A psychologist from the biological approach would consider drug therapy to be a suitable therapy as this approach follows the medical model, which suggests that mental illness is the same as physical illness, so its symptoms should be treated directly, such as through drugs. Furthermore, neurotransmitters are an assumption of the biological approach to which drug therapy directly links. This is because imbalances in neurotransmitters are thought to cause mental illnesses. Drug therapies increase transition or block receptors, to enable the therapist to alter the neurotransmitters back to 'normal'.

Examiner feedback: This student clearly refers back to the question, by applying both neurotransmitters and the medical model to the approach and therapy. This is a reasonable response in the 3–4 mark bracket. The student would not need a lot more depth to their answer to get into the top band. **4/5 marks** were awarded for this response.

Unit 2 & 4/Component 2: Scenario questions

In these questions you will be given a scenario – this is a statement about a fictional 'piece of research' – that will include information to help you respond to the questions associated with it. You should ensure that you read the scenario carefully. Use a highlighter, or just your pen, to underline key bits of information. All of the information is there for a purpose. It is your job to work out which bits of information will help you with which one of the associated questions.

A group of psychologists were interested in whether females are better at assembling flat-pack furniture than males. The psychologists used systematic sampling to select 10 females and 10 males who were shopping at a local DIY store. The flat-packs were assembled in the participants' own homes as part of a quasi-experiment.

Note: *Some of the questions following the scenario could be AO1 questions. With these questions, you do not need to refer back to the scenario:*

> *(a) Identify one difference between an experiment and a quasi-experiment.*   [1]

Advice: The differences between experiments and quasi-experiments focus on one of three things:

1. Whether the participants were randomly allocated.

2. Whether there is a control condition.

3. Whether the IV is directly manipulated.

Student Answer A

An experiment requires the participants to complete a certain task they wouldn't normally do; a quasi-experiment observes something they would already be doing.

Examiner feedback: **0/1 marks**. This is an inappropriate difference, as it is not necessarily true that the tasks in a quasi-experiment are 'something they would already be doing'.

Student Answer B

During an experiment there is the manipulation of variables by the researcher. In a quasi-experiment, there is no manipulation and it takes place during a natural environment.

Examiner feedback: **1/1 marks**. Appropriate difference identified (manipulation of variables).

(b) Briefly explain one disadvantage of an independent groups design. [2]

Advice: Disadvantages could include a lack of control over participant variables (confounding variables). There could be differences between the two groups (other than gender) that could invalidate the results, e.g. differing levels of IQ.

Student Answer A

A disadvantage is that the results would be much harder to quantify.

Examiner feedback: **0/2 marks**. This is an inappropriate disadvantage because it is not necessarily true that the results would be harder to quantify in this type of design as opposed to any other. Quantification really only applies to the type of data collected, not the way the participants were selected and therefore, the research design.

Student Answer B

Participant variables and individual differences occur. This means that there would be differences between the two groups and they would not act in the same way, therefore the results would be inconsistent.

Examiner feedback: **2/2 marks**. Disadvantage is identified and briefly explained.

from WJEC AS Paper, Unit 2, 2017

(c) Evaluate research which is conducted in the field. [6]

from WJEC AS Paper, Unit 2, 2017

Advice: This response is worth six marks; therefore, you should try to show depth and range to your answer and ensure that you are as thorough as you can be, within the time available. This answer should have BOTH advantages (such as high external validity, reduced demand characteristics, etc.) and disadvantages (lower reliability and internal validity, less control of confounding variables, etc.) of research conducted in the field. Please note that you are NOT only evaluating a field experiment, but also any research conducted in a natural environment.

Student Answer A

Field research is conducted in an everyday setting, because the results are much more likely to be valid, as they have mundane realism and are as close to real life as you can get. However, there is also very little that can be done to control the variables and therefore, the results will span widely.

Examiner feedback: **2/6 marks**. This is a basic evaluation. Two points have been made (one for and one against), but neither have any detail – bottom band response.

Student Answer B

An advantage of field research is that it is conducted in a less artificial environment, so participants' behaviour is less artificial as it is their natural environment and they are more comfortable. However, the experimenter has less control over extraneous variables, so this may affect results, reducing the reliability. Furthermore, the researcher cannot use large equipment, so not all research is viable in the field because this large equipment, such as PET scans, cannot be transported so cannot be used.

Another advantage of field research is that it has greater ecological validity as there is less manipulation than in a lab. However, this does mean that fewer causal conclusions can be drawn, as we cannot definitely say that the independent variable effected the dependent variable, or that it was other confounding variables. This is more difficult in field research, as set procedures may not be given and as a result, the research may be difficult to reproduce. Also, it is less repeatable because in a lab, standardised procedures are used so that it is reproducible.

Examiner feedback: **6/6 marks**. There is both depth and range, providing a thorough evaluation.

from WJEC AS Paper, Unit 2, 2017

TIP: Whilst this answer isn't perfect, it is enough for the marks that are allocated. Remember, you should try to find a balance by adjusting the time you spend on each question, and by considering the mark allocation.

Results from the above research were placed into a frequency table.

Female participants		Male participants	
Participant number	Time taken to complete the flat-packed furniture (in minutes)	Participant number	Time taken to complete the flat-packed furniture (in minutes)
1	105	1	83
2	92	2	72
3	78	3	100
4	87	4	63
5	62	5	68
6	110	6	79
7	98	7	84
8	200	8	96
9	85	9	101
10	73	10	94

Note: *The following questions link directly to the scenario so are AO2 questions:*

from WJEC AS Paper, Unit 2, 2017

(d) (i) *Using data from the table above, calculate the mean time taken to complete the flat-packed furniture for males and for females. Show your workings.* [2+2]

(ii) *Draw one conclusion from your calculations in part (d)(i).* [3]

(iii) *Outline one disadvantage of using the mean as a measure of central tendency to analyse this data.* [2]

Student Answer A

(i) Males = 83+72+100+63+68+79+84+96+101+94= 822 ÷ 10
= 82.2
Females = 105+92+78+87+62+110+98+200+85+73= 888 ÷ 10
= 88.8

Examiner feedback: Means given are inaccurate, but workings (showing sum of scores divided by total number of scores) are correct. **2/4 marks** awarded.

(ii) One conclusion that could be drawn is that men are quicker at assembling flat-pack furniture.

Examiner feedback: An accurate inferential conclusion is drawn (implies all men ARE quicker), but there is no link to the 'calculations in part (i)'. **1/3 marks** awarded.

(iii) One disadvantage of the mean as a measure of central tendency is that one result that is different to the others could affect the entire average. For example, one female above took 200 minutes which is 90 minutes more than the next slowest after her. This result would have an effect on the whole average.

Examiner feedback: An appropriate disadvantage is outlined and contextualised (linked to the data). **2/2 marks** awarded.

Student Answer B

(i) Males = 83+72+100+63+68+79+84+96+101+94= 840 ÷ 10
= 84
Females = 105+92+78+87+62+110+98+200+85+73= 990 ÷ 10
= 99

Examiner feedback: Means given are accurate, workings (showing sum of scores divided by total number of scores) are correct. **4/4 marks** awarded.

(ii) On average, male participants took less time than female participants. The men on average took 84 minutes, whereas the females took 99 minutes, and the average time for both males and females was 91.4 minutes.

Examiner feedback: Accurate (on average, males took less time), fully stated and linked conclusion. **3/3 marks** awarded.

TIP: If you are asked to draw a conclusion at AS, ensure that it is descriptive rather than inferential. If you quote the data and effectively 'say what you see', you will gain marks. At A level, you can use inferential conclusions where you imply results beyond the sample.

(iii) The mean does not reflect the range of values and can be easily swayed if there is a dramatic difference in one result.

Examiner feedback: an appropriate disadvantage is outlined (skew in data) but it is not contextualised (linked to the data). **1/2 marks** awarded.

Applied AO3

Unit 4 & Component 2 – Applied AO3: Refining your Personal Investigation

Whilst you can be asked to refine research from a scenario question, this type of question is most commonly found in personal investigations. As the investigations studied each year are different, it is difficult to illustrate this skill. However, if you were to take the same question as noted below and apply it to the method you used in your own investigations, a similar style of response would apply.

from Eduqas A level Paper, Component 2, 2017

INVESTIGATION TWO: An observation of gender differences in food choices.

Suggest two ways in which your own observational research could have been improved. [6]

Advice: to write an effective answer for this question you need to state an improvement. To do this, you need to make it clear what you did that needed improving first. Therefore, you should briefly say what a problem was in your research first, then say what you would change to put it right. Once you have identified the change you would make, you need to explain (in detail) how the change would make your research better – you are basically justifying your answer in context. You should use specific examples of what happened in your research and how the changes could be applied if you did the research again. Make sure that you have a logical structure, by doing one improvement at a time – you could think of it as 3 + 3 marks.

Student Answer A

My observation could have been improved if I observed the cafeteria over a longer period (e.g. a week). By just observing one lunchtime, I did not capture all students at the school, but rather a select sample that happened to be there by chance. It makes it hard to generalise the findings to all girls and boys when only a small portion of the target population was being observed.

Another area for improvement should have been observing male and female behaviour in different environments. Studies have indicated that girls of a similar age can sometimes compete with each other to be better. Therefore, in an environment that was not in school, I could have shown a different outcome where girls are less likely to display social desirability to girls in their age group.

Examiner feedback: Two quite similar suggestions for improvement, showing a 'reasonable' analysis. **4/6 marks** awarded.

TIP: Try to ensure that you make your improvements as different to one another as possible – in the case above, the candidate has basically said that the setting affected their results twice.

Student Answer B

One way my research could have been improved, is if I had expanded my sample and obtained a larger sample so that I could compare the different genders, if they were in a city or a school, or in a profession. In doing this, I could have generalised my results.

Another way my research could have been improved, is if I had paid more attention to extraneous and confounding variables. For example, I conducted my research during exam time, and during exam time, a lot of students at my sixth form would be stressed and therefore, this could act as a confounding variable, as when people are stressed, they are more likely to eat unhealthy foods that are high in sugar to give them a hit or rush of dopamine and energy.

Lastly, I would improve my food group category, because it's a very subjective scale. For example, I labelled an avocado as healthy, however, someone else may disagree and say that it's not, due to the high fat content, so I need to improve my scale so that everyone can agree on it, because if I don't, it won't be repeatable.

Examiner feedback: Three suggestions are offered when only two are required. All three were marked and then the best two were credited (the first suggestion was disregarded). The second and third suggestions are thoroughly analysed and applied to this research. **6/6 marks** awarded.

Unit 4 & Component 2 – AO2: Inferential Statistics

You will need to be able to select or justify why a specific inferential statistical test would be appropriate. To do this, you need to know (AO1) when and how they are used. If you memorise a flow chart like the one in the first section of this book (see page 22) you will be able to select an appropriate test for unseen data, should you need to (AO2).

A professor chose to investigate the following hypothesis: 'There will be a difference in the attractiveness ratings of men when they wear aftershave and when they don't wear aftershave'... The researcher invited 40 of his female students to attend the event in order to celebrate his 50th birthday.

from Eduqas AS Paper, Component 2, 2017

20 female students were randomly allocated to attend the event at 18:30 and the remaining 20 female students were asked to arrive at 20:00. 25 male students socialised with the first group of female students wearing no aftershave. After one hour the first group of female students left. The male students then applied aftershave and socialised with the second group of female students.

As they were leaving, female students were asked to give some feedback using a questionnaire. One of the questions was:

> *Using the following scale, rate the attractiveness of the male students you met at the event.*
>
> *0 – Not attractive at all*
> *1 – Weak levels of attraction*
> *2 – Reasonably attractive*
> *3 – Very attractive*

(e) The professor used a Mann-Whitney U test. Justify why this test is appropriate for analysing the data collected in this research. [4]

Advice: To gain 4 marks you have to identify all three elements/reasons why a Mann-Whitney U test would be selected, AND you have to relate each element to the scenario (AO2). If you just name the elements and do not refer to the 'data collected in this research', you can only score a maximum of 1/4 marks.

The three elements you should include are:

- Looking for a DIFFERENCE in attractiveness ratings between conditions – males with and without aftershave.

- Data is independent – two separate sets of data (independent groups), one set of scores for 20 females who rated men without aftershave and a separate set of scores for 20 different females who rated the same men with aftershave.

- Data is at least ordinal – ratings of attractiveness given by females could be placed in order on a scale of 0 – 3 (not attractive at all – very attractive).

Student Answer A

It is appropriate to use the Mann-Whitney U test, as the professor did not use nominal data, but may have used ordinal data. The study does not seek a correlation between attractiveness and aftershave, but a difference. The professor has also used an independent groups design to allocate the participants, which is required for a Mann-Whitney U test.

Examiner feedback: All three elements identified and linked to the research. Independent groups design accepted as independent data in this case. **4/4 marks.**

TIP: This was an AS level question for Eduqas students. The links to the research are quite weak, e.g. 'the professor...'. At A level you would need to be more precise and give more detail to gain full marks.

Student Answer B

It is appropriate, as the information is ordinal, and therefore compatible with the test. The numbers are also in order, which is useful.

Examiner feedback: This student refers to one possible element (ordinal data) but there is no link to the research. **0/4 marks** awarded as it's without links to the research – all three elements must be present for 1 mark.

Student Answer C

The Mann-Whitney U test is appropriate as it compares the differences of the two conditions, it involves ordinal (ordered) data and it relies on an independent groups design.

Examiner feedback: This response gives all three correct elements but has no link to the research. Maximum mark without links is **1/4 marks**.

Improved answer: The Mann-Whitney U test is appropriate as it compares the differences of the two conditions (aftershave vs no aftershave), it involves ordinal (ordered) data, such as the attractiveness ratings, and it relies on an independent groups design, where different females rate the men with and without aftershave.

(f) Using the critical values table below, select a suitable critical value that the professor should use in his analysis and explain your selection. [2]

from Eduqas AS Paper, Component 2, 2017

Table of critical values of U (p+0.05), for a two-tailed test

		N_1		
		18	19	20
	18	99	106	112
N_2	19	106	113	119
	20	112	119	127

The observed (calculated) value must be equal to or less than the critical value in this table for the result to be significant at the given level.

Advice: In this question you gain one mark for getting the correct critical value and the other for explaining why you chose it. In statistics, N or n always refers to the number of scores/participants (see page 21). We know from the scenario that there were 20 females in group 1 (no aftershave) and 20 different females in group 2 (with aftershave). This means that N1 is 20 and N2 is also 20. Reading across on the grid you can see that the critical value is therefore 127.

Student Answer A

I chose the critical value 127. As there were 40 female participants, which were split into 20 females in each group. Therefore $N_1 = 20$ and $N_2 = 20$.

Examiner feedback: The correct critical value is identified and explained. **2/2 marks.**

Student Answer B

N_2 should be used as it is a non-directional hypothesis.

Examiner feedback: Inappropriate answer given. It is a non-directional hypothesis, but the whole table is designed for a non-directional (two-tailed) test. **0/2 marks.**

Student Answer C

The critical value should be 127 because there were 20 female participants in both groups.

Examiner feedback: Appropriate critical value is identified and explained. **2/2 marks.**

TIP: As you can see, this answer is much shorter than Student Answer A, but it got an identical score. It is important in low tariff questions (like this), that you do not write too much information.

from Eduqas AS Paper, Component 2, 2017

(g) The professor found the calculated (observed) value was 123. Explain if the professor should accept or reject his null hypothesis.

[2]

Advice: In this question you would use the R up rule (discussed on page 23 of this guide – 'If there is not an R in the shortened version of the name (Sign, Wilcoxon, Mann Whitney) the rule is reversed, and to be significant, the critical value must be equal to or higher than the observed/calculated value'). However, even if you didn't know this rule, you could still answer this question. This is where reading the scenario is very important! Remember, all information is included for a reason... therefore by reading the statement below the table of critical values (*The observed (calculated) value must be equal to or less than the critical value in this table for the result to be significant at the given level*), you can work out the answer. You know that the critical value is 127 (assuming you got part (f) right) and the observed value is 123. Using the information above, you can see that the observed value IS less than the critical value and so the results ARE statistically significant at the p = 0.05 level. This means that you would accept your alternative/experimental hypothesis as there IS a difference in attractiveness between males with and without aftershave, and therefore you would reject your null hypothesis.

Student Answer A

The professor should reject the null hypothesis, as the observed value is lower than the critical value, therefore it has significance.

Examiner feedback: Correct identification and basic explanation. **2/2 marks**.

TIP: If the explanation is only worth one mark, it doesn't matter that it is basic. However, had this question been worth 3 or 4 marks, this explanation would not have been adequate.

Student Answer B

The hypothesis should be rejected as the value calculated was not equal to or less than the critical value in the table, therefore it is not significant.

Examiner feedback: Inappropriate answer given. Unfortunately, this is just wrong – the calculated value WAS less than the critical value and it WAS significant. **0/2 marks**.

Student Answer C

The professor should reject his null hypothesis.

Examiner feedback: Correctly identifies that the null should be rejected, but does not explain why. **1/2 marks**.

TIP: Do not leave questions out. With a question like this, when you have a 50/50 chance of getting it right you should always answer even if you don't know the correct response. This student has gained 1 mark for doing this and that one mark might be the difference between a grade at the end of the day.

Unit/Component 1 – AO3: Evaluate the Classic Research

In this area of evaluation, you can be asked to evaluate the methodology, procedures, findings and/or conclusions of the research. One way of going about this is to tackle evaluation thematically. Methodology and procedures are best evaluated through the terms reliability, validity and sampling. Findings and conclusions can be assessed based on their data (qualitative or quantitative), through alternative evidence (no more than two alternative studies are necessary, and NONE are actually a requirement) and social implications. Ethical considerations can be used to evaluate any aspect of the research (see page 68 for more details).

Critically evaluate Raine, Buchsbaum and LaCasse's (1997) research 'Brain abnormalities in murderers indicated by positron emission tomography'. [12]

from WJEC AS Paper, Unit 1, 2017

Advice: This question is pure evaluation. For 12 marks you have somewhere between 12–15 minutes to respond. As the question is AO3 and is worth more than 10 marks you will need to include a conclusion(s). This question requires that you evaluate the whole research and as such, any theme of evaluation is credit worthy. You should be aiming to use key terminology effectively and to show both depth and range in your response. This means that you should include multiple themes and elaborate on all of them with examples from Raine's research.

When this question was asked in the exam, the examiners were looking for evaluation along the lines of any of the below themes, but evaluation of additional relevant ideas was also creditworthy:

- Methodological Issues, e.g. use of quasi-experimental method, unable to determine cause and effect.

- Validity Issues, e.g. use of PET scans.

- Ethical Issues, e.g. valid consent, right to withdraw.

- Sampling Issues, e.g. use of murderers, control group.

- Social implications, e.g. use within the justice system.

Student Answer A

Raine et al. conducted a study on murderers who pleaded 'not guilty for reasons of insanity' (NGRI) and non-murderers. All participants were given PET scans to find out the difference in the NGRI group and non-murderers.

Raine used 41 participants in his research, 2 of which were female and 39 were male. As this is such a small sample, it is not representative of the whole population. It is also not representative due to the lack of females in the research, so the findings cannot be generalised.

All participants were from America and the NGRI group came from a prison population which again, cannot be generalised to other countries. Raine used an opportunity sample, which may be a weakness because it is not representative, however, a strength of this is that it is convenient and more representative than a random sample.

A strength of Raine's study is that there is high control, which means that the study is reliable because of the consistent results, however, the study may lack mundane realism and ecological validity and the situation doesn't truly reflect real life.

Examiner feedback: Overall this is a superficial and generic evaluation. Although it is tempting to include information about the study as an introduction (as in paragraph one), this gains no credit as it is unnecessary (it doesn't evaluate) and therefore it wastes valuable time. The remaining three paragraphs are all quite generic and all centre on sample (lacks range). The problem here is that they are not all adequately contextualised, for example, although there are more males than females in Raine's research, this is a fairly accurate representation of the prison population and murderers in general. In addition, there is nothing to suggest that murderers from the USA have brains any different to those in the rest of the world, meaning the third paragraph gains minimal credit. Moreover, the final paragraph could be about ANY study that uses an opportunity sample – it is not contextualised (**NOTE:** *using Raine's name does not count as contextualisation!*). **3/12 marks** were awarded for this response.

Student Answer B

It is possible that participants were unable to get valid consent, as they were all murderers who pleaded not guilty by reason of insanity, which suggests that they may not have been in a 'healthy' enough frame of mind to provide valid consent.

The research was conducted in a controlled environment, which means that casual conclusions can be drawn as confounding variables were controlled. It is safe to assume that the effect on the dependent variable (brain activity) was due to the independent variable (NGRI). The use of a PET scan allows researchers to study detailed regions of the brain in a way that has not been possible until recently. However, the PET scan may have caused the participants distress, an issue of psychological harm. Furthermore, the participants may not have fully understood what was expected of them during the continuous performance task (CPT), this could have lowered their self-esteem, another issue of psychological harm.

In addition, the crime was one of murder and there are many crimes that don't involve murder, therefore the findings cannot be generalised to all violent behaviour/individuals. Raine also used an opportunity sampling technique to find his sample. This is not representative, as the sample is only drawn from a small part of the target population. This lowers the validity of the research.

Raine used standardised procedures which allows the research to be replicated exactly, increasing the external reliability of the research.

Examiner feedback: Overall, there are a good range of points, most of which are well contextualised. However, the answer lacks the depth of discussion and drawing of conclusions necessary for the top band. The first two paragraphs make relevant points that are related to the study, however they both would have benefited from additional discussion to develop the points further. For example, they could have discussed the efforts Raine went to, to control other variables, to heighten the validity of his research. There is a good range of points in this response, but the last two are quite generic. **8/12 marks** were awarded for this response.

AO3

Unit/Component 1 – AO3: Evaluate the Approach

These questions can require short or longer tariff answers. Regardless of the style of question (classic evaluation or compare and contrast), there are a number of themes that you could use. One acronym that might help is DRAINS (see page 70). You could use a sandwich structure (as described on page 78) to structure your paragraphs.

from Eduqas A level Paper, Component 1, 2017

Evaluate one strength and one weakness of the cognitive approach.

[4+4]

Advice: In this question the examiner is looking for you to identify one strength/weakness, to explain why the point is strong/weak, and for you to apply the point you are making directly to the cognitive approach through examples. Using the sandwich structure described on page 78 in the first half of this guide, would ensure that all these attributes have been included.

When this question was asked in the exam, the examiners were looking for two separate paragraphs. One strength and one weakness. As the question is only worth 4 marks for each part of the question (8 in total), you do not need to include a conclusion in the response. Possible strengths/weaknesses could be based on:

- The scientific nature of the approach, e.g. the use of lab environments.

- Rejection of biological factors, e.g. lack of participation in the nature vs nurture debate.

- Determinism.

- Usefulness, e.g. how the approach has been used in therapy to improve lives.

- Success of applications, e.g. use of the approach in school, therapy, the legal system, etc.

- Reductionism, e.g. the mechanistic nature of the approach (compares humans to machines).

NOTE: *There is no exhaustive list of possible strengths/weaknesses, any relevant point is credited.*

Student Answer A

One strength of the cognitive approach is that it is scientific. Research data that has been gathered from EWT (eyewitness testimony) can be highly controlled, such as in the experiments by the Loftus and Palmer study. This allows a causal relationship to be formed between links of memory and misleading questions.

One weakness of the cognitive approach is that it ignores the nurture and nature debate, although it mentions cognitive functions of the brain, it compares it to those of a computer. It also ignores the influence of social and economic factors, which may determine a person's schemas and perceptions. This also makes it reductionist.

Examiner feedback: A strength is identified (the fact that the cognitive approach is scientific) with a superficial link to the approach – the idea of experiments such as Loftus and Palmer's research are controlled. The example is, however, muddled. **2/4 marks** for this part of the response. An appropriate weakness is also identified (the fact that the approach ignores the nature vs nurture debate), but there is no further relevant information. The point is not clearly evaluated, as some of the additional information could be considered a second weakness, e.g. the idea of reductionism. **1/4 marks** were awarded for this second part of the response.

TIP: To improve this answer the student could have used a clearer structure to their response. A better response for one strength of the cognitive approach (4 marks) could read:

One strength of the cognitive approach is that it is scientific. The cognitive approach believes that psychology is a science and as such, it should utilise scientific methodology, such as lab experiments or computer simulations. For example, Loftus and Palmer were able to control all aspects of their experiment to see the influence of one verb on their participants' estimates of speed. This suggests that the cognitive approach can make comparisons and predictions about future behaviour, because its methods are objective and can be falsified.

Student Answer B

One strength of the cognitive approach is that it gives an insight into 'mediational processes', unlike several other approaches. This means that the cognitive approach does not just focus on the stimulus-response link as a predetermination of behaviour, but also considers internal mental processes. These include memory (e.g. Atkinson and Shiffrin's multi-store model), perception and attention. Therefore, the cognitive approach acknowledges that behaviour is not just genetically predetermined (like the biological approach) or socially predetermined, but that it is governed by the way we perceive our world – this is a strength, because it provides a more holistic view on human behaviour.

However, a weakness of the cognitive approach is that it is in many ways a rather 'mechanistic approach'. For example, one assumption of the cognitive approach – the computer analogy – likens our neural processes to the functions of a computer and compares our mind's mental processes to computer hardware and software. Critics have noted that this oversimplifies human behaviour, as it does not take into account emotions – something a computer does not have. Furthermore, this potentially raises several ethical issues, such as whether machines will ever be able to function in the same way as human beings do.

Examiner feedback: This student has identified their strength and provided detailed reference to the cognitive approach, e.g. internal processes. The evaluation also provides information as to why the point made ('insight into mediational processes') is a strength of the cognitive approach ('it provides a more holistic view on human behaviour'). This evaluation point would be deemed to be thorough and accurate and as such, received **4/4 marks**. In addition, the weakness is also identified ('mechanistic approach') with a detailed reference to the cognitive approach. Evaluation towards the end explains why the point made is a weakness (where the student links the weakness to ethical issues that could arise). Again, this evaluation point received **4/4 marks**.

TIP: One reason that this student has received more marks than Student A is because of their detailed links to the approach. You should try to ensure that any evaluation paragraph (in any AO3 question) cannot be lifted into another exam response. It should be very clear which approach, therapy, method, explanation or theory your evaluation point relates to. If you could say exactly the same thing for something else, you are unlikely to gain higher marks, as your answer will not be considered to be thorough and accurate (key characteristics of a top band response). In addition, Student B has also added depth and shown understanding within their response by making comparisons to the other approaches, e.g. '...behaviour is not just genetically predetermined (like the biological approach) ...' This kind of comment shows a true insight into the approach and how it differs to its counterparts, something that would be particularly useful within a compare and contrast style AO3 response. That said, you should apply caution when using this technique. If the student had only used these types of comparisons but didn't provide specific examples of the cognitive approach within their response, they would not have written an effective answer. This means that it is highly recommended that you learn some core examples from each approach that you could use to 'stick' your evaluation, so that it is no longer 'floaty' like a cloud (see page 71 for more detailed examples of how to make answers 'sticky').

AO3

Unit/Component 2 – AO3: Social and Developmental Psychology

On Unit/Component 2 you can be asked about social and developmental psychology through two key studies; Milgram's (1963) research into obedience and Kohlberg's (1968) research into moral development. Milgram is social psychology, whilst Kohlberg is developmental. Social psychology concerns research conducted into topics such as social conformity/influence (Asch and/or Zimbardo) and obedience (Milgram), whereas developmental psychology concerns research conducted into child development (Kohlberg, Bowlby and to a lesser extent, Freud).

from Eduqas AS Paper, Component 2, 2016

Research conducted by social psychologists, such as Milgram, often has ethical issues. Analyse ethical issues that arise in social psychological research. [10]

Advice: Analyse means to evaluate through examples. To gain a top band mark (8–10 marks) you would need to: Include a range of ethical issues (more than one), use examples from Milgram's research (or the research of other social psychologists, e.g. Zimbardo or Asch), utilise core terminology surrounding ethical issues, and give an appropriate conclusion. In an ideal world, you would use the sandwich structure where you identify the ethical issue, you talk about why it's a problem, you give examples from social psychology, and you create a mini conclusion about why this issue is problematic. You would repeat this process for each issue before concluding.

When this question was asked in the exam, the examiners were looking for an analysis of any ethical issue common to social psychological research. Answers could include analysis of:

- Valid consent.

- Deception.

- Risks of stress, anxiety, humiliation or pain.

- Any other relevant issue that is contextualised.

Student Answer A

Informed consent is usually an issue because when investigating social research, in order to not get socially desirable/invalid results, the participants can't know the real aim of the study, so the results remain valid. Although, to stay within ethical guidelines, they must be told enough about the study in order to get any consent and have a debrief showing the true aim of the study.

Deception is usually an issue because the researcher needs to make sure that ethical guidelines are met, although some deception is allowed. An example of this involves Milgram's experiment, as he told the participants the electric shock machine was real when it wasn't, although if he hadn't done this, the study wouldn't have been valid as the experiment wouldn't work properly or have any mundane realism.

Harm to participants can be an issue, as the experiments must have some ecological validity to be realistic, in order to make the results valid. Researchers may not always expect any harm to occur. For example, before Milgram's study took place, many psychologists said the participants would not follow the orders, although the findings showed that all participants reached 300v. Because of this Milgram couldn't have been expected to know that any psychological harm would occur as in other social psychological research. After the experiment, Milgram did take precautions to ensure that their psychological state was the same as before the experiment.

Examiner feedback: Ethical issues are largely described rather than analysed. There is 'reasonable' use of Milgram's research, but no other examples of social psychology are included. There is no conclusion in regards to ethical issues in social psychological research, which is required in applied evaluation. **4/10 marks**.

TIP: To improve this response the candidate should have used evaluative language. If they had made it clear which points were strengths (like Milgram ensuring the participant's psychological state was the same at the end of the study as at the beginning) and weaknesses (deception about the electric shocks), this would have improved their answer. They could have included other knowledge of alternative research within social psychology. It is highly likely that most students will have heard of Zimbardo. This would have been an ideal opportunity to include his work.

Student Answer B

One ethical issue that arises in social psychology research is using vulnerable individuals as the participants. This will include children, adults with mental illnesses and elderly people with dementia. This could cause an issue of valid consent, as the individuals may not fully understand what they are taking part in and therefore, cannot give fully informed consent. To combat this issue, parents or carers could give valid consent for the individual.

A second issue is of working with animals, as there are many ethical guidelines. Animals cannot give valid consent to deal with this issue. The researchers are asked to try to avoid the use of animals in research and instead use alternatives, such as computer simulators. If using animals is completely unavoidable, the research must use the minimum number of animals, in order to reduce any risks. Professional vets and animal experts should also be present throughout the study, in case their assistance is required.

Other ethical issues include privacy, confidentiality, deception, risk of harm and valid consent.

Examiner feedback: This answer is largely not relevant (the whole second paragraph is not relevant to social psychology – as social psychology focuses on the interaction between humans). Some ethical issues have been identified, but none have been analysed. **1/10 marks** awarded.

NOTE: *This question was answered quite poorly by several candidates. The mean score across all candidates was only 4.9/10. That's only half the marks – therefore, this question has been addressed in more detail in the student workbook, that can be used alongside this guide.*

Unit 2/Component 1 – AO1/3: Contemporary Debates

AO1/3

These questions have an equal amount of AO1 and AO3 marks available and require you to create a 'debate' or argument between the two main perspectives. AO1 (knowledge) marks are allocated to the examplars of psychological theory and research that you include within your debate. AO3 (evaluation) marks are allocated to your discussion and debating skills. Links to the question stem (including any statement or quote) are all marked as AO3. In addition, comments about social, economic and ethical implications of the debate are credited under this AO. Furthermore, your conclusion(s) make up a significant part of your AO3 score.

Discuss the use of conditioning techniques to control the behaviour of children, including ethical and social implications. [20]

from WJEC AS Paper, Unit 2, 2017

NOTE: *For A level in England (Eduqas) this same question would be worth 24 marks not 20.*

Advice: In this question the examiner was looking for you to understand why using conditioning techniques with children is a debate. You should not just write about when it has been used, but you should ideally show an appreciation of WHY conditioning should or should not be utilised to 'control the behaviour of children'. This debate centres on whether it is moral, ethical and justified to manipulate children's behaviour – yes we accept that we 'can', but should we? Debates are marked across AO1 and AO3: to write an effective answer, you are aiming to carefully select and use exemplars to support the points you make (AO1). AO3 (evaluation) marks are allocated to your discussion and debating skills. In addition, comments about social and ethical implications of the debate are credited as AO3. Do not forget to include a conclusion!

When this question was asked in the exam, the examiners were looking for a debate: arguments for and against using conditioning on kids. Possible themes for discussion could be based on:

- Conditioning at home.

- Conditioning in schools.

- Conditioning with children who have special educational needs.

How each of these link to ethical and/or social implications should also be included in your response.

Student Answer A

Conditioning techniques can be used by parents on their children. Jo Frost, The 'Supernanny' used techniques in her show such as the naughty step to give disobedient children a positive punishment. This is so the children do not repeat the behaviour that caused the punishment. However, many argue that this is unethical. Children don't have the same ability as adults to reflect on their behaviour, so all this punishment does is cause psychological harm. This may last throughout the child's life, causing problems later on in life.

Another idea is that conditioning techniques can be used in school through token economies. Here, teachers give students positive reinforcements (gold stars) so that they repeat good behaviours. Lefrancois said that more positive reinforcement (pretty classrooms, friendly comments) with less negative reinforcement (removing shouting and criticism) is beneficial for children in school. However, it was also found that children perform worse under such conditions due to complacency. People praised for their results on a test did worse on the next test than those who were criticised. This is learned helplessness.

As children get older, they tend to copy the behaviours of their peers in order to fit in. This has bad implications, as research has shown that children as young as 10 are more likely to drink and smoke if their friends do. This is bad for society and unhealthy for the child. Conditioning techniques can also be used on vulnerable children, such as those with autistic spectrum disorder.

In conclusion, conditioning techniques are dangerous when used by a child's peers, but beneficial when given by a parent or teacher to improve behaviour.

Examiner feedback: **9/20 marks** were awarded in total.
AO1: 4/10 Exemplars (Supernanny, positive reinforcement and the idea of conditioning in the classroom) are basic. Inherent

knowledge is clear, e.g. discussion of Lefrancois, but is not always well applied. There is some range and detail in ideas that is better than superficial, but still basic. Information on peers (Social Learning Theory) is not well related to the question, as it is not a form of conditioning.

AO3: 5/10 Basic discussion of both sides of the debate – weak links to benefits of conditioning in schools and parenting – better discussion of ethical concerns/limitations.

TIP: One way this answer could have been improved is by elaborating on some of their relevant points better. For example, the candidate mentions conditioning techniques with vulnerable children, but this is not extended or explained – this would increase their score. In addition, their conclusion could have done with the purpose of the debate being drawn together in a better way.

Student Answer B

The use of conditioning techniques to control the behaviour of children is a controversial debate within psychology. Some may argue that such manipulation of behaviour is unethical, whereas others suggest that it is needed to create a desirable society. There is plenty of research both for and against the use of conditioning techniques, especially when it comes to children within the education system.

Conditioning techniques to control behaviour is promoted by Supernanny Jo Frost, who uses the technique of the 'naughty step'. She suggests that when parents shout at their children, although such attention is unpleasant, it actually positively reinforces the behaviour. So, in order to deal with this, parents must stop reinforcement. The Supernanny team techniques, such as the naughty step, aid in stopping such behaviour. However, a naughty step has been criticised by many as having a negative effect on the emotional development of the child, because at such a young age, children do not possess the ability to reflect on their behaviour and express their emotions about such a technique. There is also the issue of consistency – the technique is not likely to work as effectively as what is claimed by the experts, because many parents will experience stressful times with work, so may appear frustrated or be inconsistent whilst using the technique, which diminishes the effectiveness of it. When considering this particular aspect of conditioning it is easy to see how using such a technique on children may hinder, rather than aid the child's development and behaviour.

Conditioning techniques are often used in the education system through the means of operant conditioning, e.g. the use of gold stars to positively reinforce good behaviour and academic performance. Such use is considered normal in today's society and appears to work with encouraging positive behaviour. A study suggests that increasing the use of teacher praise and disapproval leads to a better work performance in an English class in a high school. Also, by adding pleasant stimulus, such as a wall display and laughter, and removing unpleasant stimuli, such as shouting, children had a more positive attitude to their work and their performance improved.

On the other hand, research by a psychologist suggests otherwise, as children who were promised a reward on completion of a drawing, spent only half of the time drawing, compared to the children who were not promised a reward. It is important to consider therefore, how such reward-based conditioning could diminish the internal motivation of children, and could make society less cohesive and more selfish.

Another key part of this debate is the use of conditioning techniques on vulnerable children. Some argue that using such techniques may help 'normalise' behaviour and help them learn to participate fully within society, such as becoming employed. However, it is important to question the ethicality of this and to question also what is deemed as normal and desirable behaviour.

To conclude, conditioning techniques to control children may have economic gains, such as increasing performance academically, but may also have drawbacks, such as schools' limited budgets to pay for such rewards. This is combined also with the ethical question of whether it is acceptable to spend such money rewarding children for achievements, when it could be better spent elsewhere. Overall, conditioning techniques are proven to be effective if used correctly and consistently, but may have implications on a child's development, if not used properly.

Examiner feedback: **18/20 marks** were awarded in total.

AO1: 8/10 Exemplars are appropriate and show a reasonable level of accuracy. There is depth and range to the material. Understanding of examples used is highlighted through discussion points but named psychological studies or support would have lifted this answer.

AO3: 10/10 Discussion is thorough and evaluative comments refer to social and ethical implications throughout the answer. The conclusion is appropriate (additional mini conclusions are used throughout) and are based on the evidence presented.

AO2/3

Unit/Component 3 – AO2/3: Controversies

There are five different controversies: Cultural bias, ethical costs of conducting research, non-human animals, scientific status and sexism (in some schools/colleges you will only learn four out of five). For each controversy you need to understand the issue at hand and know why it is considered controversial – Why is there debate in this topic? AO2 in these questions refers to the application of evidence, so each time you use a core idea/theme/piece of research you will be awarded AO2 marks if you have linked it to the question in hand. Any links to the statement/quote (if there is one), are also AO2. AO3 is your discussion of the controversy. Use of evaluative language, creating a clear argument, developing your points so that the debate is well balanced and carefully concluding the debate, are all important if you want to gain a high score.

from Eduqas A level Paper, Component 3, 2017

'Psychology is a science.' Using your knowledge of psychology, discuss the extent to which this statement is true. **[25]**

Advice: In a controversies question that encompasses the whole debate (like the one above), rather than focusing on one specific area of exploration, you SHOULD be able to excel. All information you have learned is relevant across all four areas of exploration. Therefore, it is your job to create a logical flow of information that utilises all of your knowledge and draws a clear conclusion in relation to the question stem – Is psychology a science? If the evidence suggests it is, then you will suggest that the statement is 'true', if the evidence suggests it isn't, then you will suggest that the statement is NOT true at the end of the essay. It is essential in a controversies question that you draw specific conclusions about the controversy and, where possible, you explain, through your response, why the issue is controversial.

Likely content for discussion will include:

- Exploration of the four themes: benefits of being a science, changing nature of 'science', costs of being a science and the methodologies of the approaches.

- Comparisons of methodologies employed by science and psychology.

- Principles/characteristics of science compared to the various psychological approaches.

- Impact of studying humans as test subjects.

Student Answer A

Science is when research is conducted to prove a theory or hypothesis in an objective and controlled manner, as the results produced are valid and reliable and can be replicated.

Psychology is a science because it brings many social and economic benefits to society. For psychology to be a science it has to prove theories and hypothesises, e.g. a man is more aggressive than a woman or drugs can treat a disorder. These theories, if they weren't tested, would be ineffective and the sample of participants used has to be generalisable to society for it to be useful. Psychology has tested many theories in an ethical manner that has proved useful to society, e.g. drug therapy has saved the NHS £22.5 billion per year.

However, to a lesser extent psychology is not a science, as a science aims to prove a cause and effect between two variables, which it cannot do due to multiple factors influence. For example, schizophrenia has multiple explanations and it is difficult to draw cause and effect which leads to causal conclusions.

Furthermore, to some extent psychology is a science because it can use a range of methodologies to make results replicable which makes it high on reliability, e.g. brain scans. This is done through triangulation – combining more than one methodology. This makes the research more objective than subjective so more quantitative data is produced, which is easier to manipulate, and it is easier to use various statistical tests to analyse the data.

However, to a lesser extent psychology is not a science because even though there is no cause and effect demonstrated, the conclusions from research should be interpreted with caution and should not be taken literally. This is because individuals are different, and everyone has factors that can cause an effect, and not the so called 'cause'. Such cause and effect demonstrated in psychology can be negative socially. For example, James Fallon used a series of brain scans to show the brain structures of criminal schizophrenics, compared to normal people. Information shown in this research could have been interpreted quite literally so essentially, everyone could have had their brain scanned and have a similar structure to a criminal schizophrenic who would be put into prison. However, multiple factors were considered, as Fallon showed that he had a brain of a schizophrenic, but due to nurture – his upbringing – it was not triggered.

In addition, psychology is not a science because there are various pieces of research that only include literature reviews or self-report that has low replicability and ecological validity, e.g. Myers and Diener 'who is happy?' was based on self-report, and literature review. This lacked scientific status as it had low generalisability and could not be compared to other studies or compared within the study as there were many differences that weren't comparable, e.g. society, social norms, economy, ethically.

Overall, psychology is a science because it provides objective and reliable data that can be generalised and can be compared against. However, psychology is not a science because no cause and effect can be drawn in most situations and multiple factors have to be considered.

Examiner feedback: The candidate makes varied attempts to provide links back to the statement. Evidence/comments made are not always made clearly relevant to the title and statement, and expression of some points is unclear – with some issues not being explained accurately. The candidate clearly did attempt to evaluate, but they do not engage in any great depth with the issue. For example, making use of actual studies to illustrate, or not, the nature of science in psychology. Using theory/explanation to further reinforce points would be useful. In addition, reference to Kuhn and/or Popper, notable advocates of argument in this area, is also a significant omission to the nature of evaluation in this debate. **AO2: 5/10 AO3: 6/15 = 11/25 marks.**

Student Answer B

In psychology, a lot of research is conducted to explain certain types of behaviour. These explanations are split into the five schools of psychology. With reference to these approaches, I will be discussing the extent to which psychology is scientific and is to be considered a science.

Psychology cannot be considered a science when looking at the psychodynamic approach. This is due to the fact that in certain areas of psychology, statements are made which can't be falsified. For example, in the psychodynamic approach, Freud mentions the tripartite personality and how there is the id, ego and superego. However, there is no evidence to show that they truly exist. Even if Bowlby and the 44 thieves serves as scientific research, it does not prove that the id, ego and superego exist, and so the approach makes psychology unscientific and so can't be called a science.

However, the biological approach makes psychology scientific as there are means of testifying the impact of neurotransmitters and brain scans in which results can be made replicable and reliable, such as Raine (2004), where CAT scans are used to analyse the activity of the brain in relation to aggression. This approach makes psychology, to an extent, scientific and therefore a science.

On the other hand, psychology can be considered as not scientific as many views in psychology are biased. An example is Kohlberg's reasoning for moral stages of development. Kohlberg himself chooses a sample of 75 American males and uses his own judgement to deem what is morally right or wrong. Therefore, it makes his view biased and affects his overall research. There is also gender bias which contributes to the fact that Kohlberg believed in male supremacy and so regarded that his results would be the same for females without testing it. This makes psychology unscientific and not considered a science as the approaches are influenced by the beliefs of certain psychologists.

In contrast, it can be considered scientific when looking at studies which use a matched pairs design as well as inter-rater reliability. A study on the effect of a drug was seen by matching patients to other patients of similar age, sex and medical condition, before using more than one doctor to analyse the results, therefore increasing inter-rater reliability. The use of experimental design in psychology makes it scientific and therefore we can call psychology a science due to the fact that research has standardised procedures set by the BPS to make sure it is scientific to pass as reliable research.

In conclusion, you can say that there are many aspects of psychology that make it scientific to some extent, such as the use of experimental design and in some cases, lab settings to test for a hypothesis/aim which is standardised in all research for psychology. However, the fact that research can be biased, unethical (for example Milgram) and the influence of theories that can't be falsified, makes psychology less scientific and more idealistic. The influence of psychologists such as Freud on the psychodynamic approach and Kohlberg creating his own idealistic stages using his own views on morality, make psychology less realistic and therefore more biased and not scientific. Therefore, psychology cannot be called a science.

Examiner feedback: The response by this candidate illustrates that the evidence selected for use was appropriate. The candidate has ensured that in some cases, clear references back to the statement are given, but this is not apparent in all cases – hence 'reasonable' references to the statement are made (AO2). The candidate makes a range of points but could have improved the response by adding detail (depth), elaborating further on the points made. The candidate has tried throughout the essay to engage with the debate. The use of evaluation terminology is apparent. To this extent, the candidate has provided a thorough interpretation of the key issue. There is a balanced discussion, with recognition of both sides of the debate. The structure is appropriate for the response and a conclusion is provided which does respond to the question set.

AO2: 7/10 AO3: 10/15 = 17/25 marks.